KU-466-014

PELICAN BOOKS
A619
AMERICAN CAPITALISM
J. K. GALBRAITH

# J. K. GALBRAITH

# *American Capitalism*

## THE CONCEPT OF
## COUNTERVAILING POWER

PENGUIN BOOKS
IN ASSOCIATION WITH
HAMISH HAMILTON

Penguin Books Ltd, Harmondsworth, Middlesex
AUSTRALIA: Penguin Books Pty Ltd, 762 Whitehorse Road,
Mitcham, Victoria

—

First published in the U.S.A. 1952
This revised edition first published in the U.S.A. 1956
and in Great Britain by Hamish Hamilton 1957
Published in Pelican Books 1963

—

Copyright © J. K. Galbraith, 1952 and 1956

—

Made and printed in Great Britain
by C. Nicholls & Company Ltd
Set in Monotype Plantin

This book is sold subject to the condition
that it shall not, by way of trade, be lent,
re-sold, hired out, or otherwise disposed
of without the publisher's consent,
in any form of binding or cover
other than that in which
it is published

*For Douglas*

# CONTENTS

# FOREWORD

AMONG the problems in which a book such as this involves its author there are three which I feel I should share with the reader. The first concerns the hideous chance of war. The ideas here offered I first worked out in the years following the Second World War when it seemed possible to assume that the world would be for a while at peace. This assumption was rudely jolted a year before the first edition went to press by the outbreak of the Korean War. The opening paragraphs of that edition warned that these ideas had little meaning for a United States at war and that they would not seem very relevant when viewed from the radioactive debris that would remain after a war, including a victorious one.

Since the book first appeared, the threat of war has seemed at times to increase and at other times to ebb. There have been occasions when statesmen have come close to implying that there might be something rather noble about sudden, massive, and very high-temperature extinction. On other occasions they have seemed to sense that this programme might not be popular with the average voter. While, if anything, the prospects for peace have grown better rather than worse, it is doubtful if the threat of war will entirely disappear in our time. So it is necessary to continue to make explicit the assumption of peace – the assumption, as noted, on which this excursion into social comment is based – and to hope that it is well founded. If the assumption is ill founded, problems of economics will not soon again be discussed on as amiable a plane as here.

My second problem was much less portentous. It concerned the idiom in which one should write a book such as this. I have, especially in the latter chapters, a great many things to say to my fellow economists. I am proud to be counted a professional economist; I consider economics a progressive as well as a distinguished subject matter. Yet I would not have written this book had I not felt that some of the conclusions now reached by my professional colleagues are quite wrong. Anyone so unfortunately persuaded should, normally, address his writing to his fellows. There are many advantages in this. Economics has developed a shorthand terminology which, however baffling it may be to the layman, has great advantages in speed and ease of communication for the initiated. It requires a certain precision of thought and statement which is a protection against careless thinking and which places critics on firm ground in recognizing and protesting error. It also assures the critics that the author is learned in the terminology of his subject.

All these good reasons notwithstanding, I early decided to address this book to the lay reader – and to appeal to my critics to believe that I could be incomprehensible had I wished. I felt sufficiently confident of the ideas to want to seek a general audience. As a result, though there are some things here which the diligent layman may find implausible, there is little that he will fail to understand.

In writing as I have, it has been necessary to simplify a good many matters. My competitive model is a stripped design and students of the history of economic thought will miss many refinements. I have especially simplified and abbreviated that part of the Keynesian doctrine of savings and investment which I needed for my purpose. But simplification can be of two kinds. It can be a matter of convenience which leads to conclusions that are based on the full content of truth. Or it can lead to error. My simplification is intended to be of the first sort. If any is of the second sort I am to be held accountable.

Third, I have had to contend, as I imagine have many others, with the problem of how to designate, with reasonable brevity, the differing political attitudes of Americans on economic issues. In a book like this the line between economics and politics must truly be an imaginary one – it is a parallel that must be crossed and recrossed without consultation even with the reader. In the United Kingdom there are Socialists and Tories and when one uses these political labels to designate a group of people one indicates fairly accurately the political views and temperament of those designated. Needless to say, with us party labels convey no similar meaning.

In our time the ancient and useful distinction between Left and Right has developed a colour which also makes it nearly useless. To many the notion of the 'Left' connotes some alignment, direct or vague, with communism and in any case there is an old tendency to associate it with political positions derived from Marx. The 'Right' for many has become synonymous with blind reaction. Accordingly these terms bear not on the reality but on the pathology of our political life and with the latter I am not much concerned.

My solution has been to follow W. S. Gilbert and classify all men as liberal or conservative – if not by birth at least by temperament and the effects of circumstance. This, at least, has the sanction of long usage. So far as the American conservative is concerned, it presents no serious difficulty. American conservatism has the unifying characteristic of dislike of change. It does divide as to tactics – as between those who resist change *qua* change, which is perhaps the normal pattern of our conservatism, and those who accept limited change to protect the broad contours of the past and present.

The use of the term liberal raises far more questions – almost as many as it answers. In Europe the term has a clear political content: the continental liberal is, and simply, an opponent of government intervention in the economy. In practice, this means resistance to any interference with vested positions of privilege or monopoly as well as to any and all forms of state-sponsored planning. There are Americans who regard themselves as liberals in this sense, but not many. American liberalism is far more likely to view improvement in welfare and also an attack on vested position as its central tasks and to accept, or indeed seek, whatever state intervention it believes to be required for these ends. The best one can do with the term, as we use it, is to assume such an attitude coupled with a general predisposition towards change. After all, it is one of the distinctive features of American liberalism that on economic matters both its methods and its goals are exceedingly diverse. When a basket is filled with a great many different vegetables, one should not strain to say that it contains only potatoes.

Let me add that I think the reader will find this a good-humoured book. There is a place, no doubt, for the great polemic – for the volume that assails with unmitigated fury the ideas, interests, morals, and motives of all unfortunates, the quick and the dead, who happen to be in the author's path. I am not capable of such anger; I would like to suppose that I do not take myself so seriously. In any case this is a method which probably serves better the purposes of politics and evangelism than of enlightenment.

Yet this is an essay in social criticism. The task of criticism is criticism. I pass under review ideas that are strongly held and positions that are warmly defended and, with some, at least, I take vigorous issue. Even though they are, as here, the ideas of men I respect, this is the way of progress. And such criticism is especially important in economics. Like theology, and unlike mathematics, economics deals with matters which men consider very close to their lives. There has always been a tendency for its ideas to crystallize into dogma; neither liberals nor conservatives have a very good record of weighing challenges to accepted concepts and doctrines with critical detachment. Accordingly, one of the most important and difficult of the responsibilities of the economist is to resist the authority of the accepted.

The present volume is a substantial revision of the edition which first appeared in the spring of 1952. The changes are of several kinds. Some things in the first edition had relevance only to their time and these have been deleted. With time some other things have changed. (In the preface to the first edition I cited Senator Wayne Morse of Oregon as an example of the irregularity allowed to a member of the Republican Party. He has since become a Democrat.) Much more important, the rather considerable discussion of these ideas since they were first offered has convinced me that in some instances I was wrong and in others that, either through brevity or ambiguity, I had conveyed the wrong impression. Here I have corrected myself.

A number of these corrections, as might be expected, have to do with the chapters on countervailing power. However, I have made more extensive revisions in the last two chapters which, in their original form, reflected unduly the economic context of the Korean War in which they were written.

In spite of these changes the substance of the original argument remains and indeed, I trust, is strengthened. This will be a sad disappointment to those generous people who have laboured so hard to argue me out of these heresies and who have sought to extirpate the notion of countervailing power from the otherwise pure stream of economic thought. I am grateful to them none the less. I think I have been made wiser by their efforts. I confess that I am even more grateful to those who have given their general approval to this argument.

# CHAPTER I

# The Insecurity of Illusion

I

IT is told that such are the aerodynamics and wing-loading of the bumblebee that, in principle, it cannot fly. It does, and the knowledge that it defies the august authority of Isaac Newton and Orville Wright must keep the bee in constant fear of a crack-up. One can assume, in addition, that it is apprehensive of the matriarchy to which it is subject, for this is known to be an oppressive form of government. The bumblebee is a successful but an insecure insect.

If all this be true, and its standing in physics and entomology is perhaps not of the highest, life among the bumblebees must bear a remarkable resemblance to life in the United States in recent years. The present organization and management of the American economy are also in defiance of the rules – rules that derive their ultimate authority from men of such Newtonian stature as Bentham, Ricardo, and Adam Smith. Nevertheless there are occasions – the decade following the Second World War was an example – when it works, and quite brilliantly. The fact that it does so, in disregard of precept, has caused men to suppose that all must end in a terrible smash. And, as with the bee, there is frequently a deep concern over the intentions of those in authority. This also leads to apprehension and insecurity.

It is with this insecurity, in face of seeming success, that this book, in the most general sense, is concerned. The favourable performance of the American economy in the years following the Second World War was a fact. There were some two million farm families, many of them in the southern Appalachians, who continued to live in a primitive and anonymous squalor not surpassed in any country west of Turkey. There were urban slum dwellers and racial minorities, notably the Negroes, who could not view their lot with satisfaction. The same was true of those whose salaries, pensions, or dependence on past savings committed them to life on a fixed income. Elsewhere there was little hardship. Nor, so far as one can judge, did the generality of Americans feel that their personal freedom had been seriously abridged. The ideas which caused the present to be viewed with such uncertainty, and the future with such alarm, were not operative. My purpose is to see why – and perhaps to learn how, if we are spared – these ideas can be kept inoperative.

II

That the success of the economy in the years following the Second World War was accompanied by deep uneasiness is a point that need hardly be laboured. Undoubtedly the uneasiness was greatest among businessmen. These were years of high production and generous profits. Business had recovered much of the prestige it had lost during the depression; even at election time it was again being treated with marked courtesy by the government.

Yet there was little evidence that businessmen, or more especially their leaders, viewed their prospects with equanimity. On the contrary, the tone of business statements during these years was often that of a communiqué promising a last-ditch stand against disaster. This was especially so prior to the Republican victory in the autumn of 1952. Thus, in early 1948 the weekly organ of the nation's leading business organization, the *NAM News*, observed that the President's State of the Union Message promised 'impossible burdens' for business and quoted, approvingly, the view of unnamed conservative politicians that, if enacted, the programme 'would first hobble and then ultimately destroy the American business system'. A few weeks later, in March, the same journal reported that the president of the Association had taken to the road to spread 'industry's ideas and ideals in the unremitting battle against totalitarianism'. This it should be noted was totalitarianism at home, not abroad, and having carried his 'plea for freedom' to Kansas City he proceeded to Houston, Shreveport, and New Orleans, where he warned that the 'threat to American freedom is unremitting.' A year later his successor told a Jacksonville audience that 'at the highest level of prosperity, our people have lost faith in freedom and are moving away from it.' An Association editorial sombrely observed that 'millions who yield to no one in their zeal to advance the national welfare are seriously concerned lest what we struggle against on a world-wide basis creep upon us at home without our realizing it. They believe we will drift into Statism. ...' President Truman's new message to the Congress was subsequently viewed with alarm. Early in 1950 the Chamber of Commerce of the United States, in an attractively printed brochure entitled *Socialism in America*, warned, urgently, against the 'back road to socialism'. It drew attention to the then recently expressed fears of Mr James F. Byrnes, former Supreme Court Justice, Senator and Secretary of State, that the people of the United States could 'be led over a bridge of socialism into a police state'.

This pessimism is subject to considerable discount even by businessmen themselves. On 21 April 1950, at a luncheon meeting in Baltimore the President of the United States Steel Corporation made the apocalyptic declaration that the American economic system was 'in deadlier peril than it has ever been in my lifetime'. The stock market rose moderately in late trading and Steel Common was up a quarter for the day. A prominent business spokesman conceded at the 1949 meeting of the National Association of Manufacturers that businessmen were in the vanguard of gloom. The people, at large, he declared, were 'apathetic and complacent ... too busy playing golf, or looking at television, or tending to their businesses, to protect the freedom and opportunity which have made America what it is.' In 1953, moreover, the appearance in Washington, after twenty long years of an avowedly pro-business administration did something to reduce anxiety. In the autumn of 1953 Mr Sinclair Weeks, the Secretary of Commerce, was able to report to the annual meeting of the National Association of Manufacturers that 'a climate favourable to business has most definitely been substituted for the socialism of recent years.' Not everyone was reassured, however. Two years later the newly installed president of the Association, a Wisconsin paper manufacturer, advised the assembled delegates that 'creeping socialism is now walking.' He adduced evidence in support of the advanced conclusion that 'we're already well on our way to the achievement of the Communist State as blueprinted by Marx.'

The notion that American capitalism* is a fragile and evanescent thing has a strong grip on the minds of many citizens. The principal and, apart from treason, the all but exclusive issue in elections since the war has been whether America is being transformed from a capitalist into a welfare state, a statist state, or a socialist one. Early in 1950 the Republican Party formally resolved to fight its next election campaign on the issue of 'liberty versus socialism'. The Honorable Jesse W. Wolcott of Michigan was able to give a precise arithmetical measure to the

---

* For many years this term, which denotes that the men who own the business, or those who are directly or indirectly their agents, have a major responsibility for decision, has been regarded as vaguely obscene. All sorts of euphemisms – free enterprise, individual enterprise, the competitive system, and the price system – are currently used in its place. None of them has the virtue of being more descriptive and none is as succinct.

imminency of revolution. 'The United States is now within eight per cent of socialism,' he told an audience of real estate men in late 1949. The President of Columbia University, soon to become President of the United States, in sending his flock into the world in 1949 was less quantitative but scarcely less urgent. 'In the years ahead of you graduates, the fundamental struggle of our time may be decided – between those who would further apply to our daily life the concept of individual freedom and equality; and those who would subordinate the individual to the dictates of the state. . . .'

III

The businessman shares with many others yet another fear which, unlike his political doubts, he leaves largely unexpressed. It is that private capitalism is inherently unstable. For full five years after the Japanese surrender in 1945, nearly every mature and prudently conducted business in the United States was guided by the assumption that, at some time in the future, the United States would have a serious depression. The postwar inventory, dividend and reserve policies of American corporations, and the jagged behaviour of the stock market in face of record incomes and yields become comprehensible only when the depth and breadth of that alarm is recognized. With time and continuing prosperity the fear of depression has been blunted. It is a ghost, however, which still haunts the board rooms. Good times may last out this year and next, but obviously we are going to have a smash one of these days.

In accordance with a surprisingly well-observed convention, the American business spokesman does not often express his fear of depression in public. To express the fear is, perhaps, to invite the fact – and perhaps also to inspire the interest of the state in measures to counter the threat. Few others have been under such a ban. Farmers, workers, and intellectuals, in the years since the war, have made no secret of their fear of depression. Before the Second World War ended it was taken as accepted that there would be a postwar collapse with unemployment ranging upward from seven, eight, or ten millions. What was called postwar planning consisted almost exclusively in planning for such a disaster. The postwar guarantees of farm prices, the large public works programmes that were projected, and the Employment Act of 1946 all tacitly assumed such a collapse.

The case of the farmers is especially instructive. In the decade following the war Congress was almost continuously concerned with farm legislation, immediate or prospective. Until almost the end of the decade few farmers – few, at least, of those whose voices are heard in Washington – were gravely dissatisfied with the prices and incomes they were receiving. On the contrary several were bonanza years such as few farmers had ever dreamed of seeing. But it was taken for granted by farmers that American capitalism would one day return to its normal pattern of performance. For most this was a simple portrait of its behaviour during the nineteen-thirties. To protect themselves in that collapse of capitalism, they were enthusiastically advocating and enacting the comprehensive controls over their price and production which conservatives saw as the antithesis of capitalism.

IV

The liberal, following the war, shared, and did not hesitate to voice, the conservative's conviction that American capitalism is unstable with a strong bias towards depression. He had further causes for disquiet. As the conservative worried about government power so the liberal was alarmed over business power. In what I shall presently argue is a normal pattern of capitalist organization, a large share of the productive activity

20

of the United States is carried on by a comparatively small number of corporations. Agricultural production, much trade and, subject to some underlying control of production and prices by trade unions, the mining of soft coal and the manufacture of clothing are still in the hands of the small firms. Much though not all of the rest is in the domain of the giants; the heads of the corporations that produce between a third and a half of the national product of the United States could be seated comfortably in almost any neighbourhood motion-picture theatre.

This is not new. It is possible that the hundred largest corporations did nearly as great a proportion of the business of the United States in 1905 as today. It was only in the thirties, however, that the extent of this concentration was measured with passable thoroughness. The statistics converted what had been a suspicion into a conviction.

There is no place in the liberal's system for these vast administrative units. The large corporation can have significant power over the prices it charges, over the prices it pays, even over the mind of the consumer whose wants and tastes it partly synthesizes. There is nothing in the American tradition of dissent so strong as the suspicion of private business power. It produced the Sherman Act, a nearly unique effort to shape the growth of capitalism, the Wilsonian efforts to extend its effectiveness, the colourful lawsuits of Thurman Arnold in the late thirties, and the liberal lawyer's undiluted enthusiasm for antitrust enforcement.

In spite of all these efforts – and apparently the statistics now left no room for comforting disbelief – big business had triumphed. No plausible doctrine was available, even to conservatives, which led to the conclusion that the undisturbed exercise of its power would be for the common good. On the contrary the accepted doctrine held that, via monopoly, it led to social inefficiency and to oppression. The optimism of the

American liberal as to what might be accomplished by the antitrust laws has always been great. For the first time it now became necessary for him to wonder if even the antitrust laws could alter the existing structure of the American economy. If not, big business and its power were here to stay. To his uneasiness over power for which he had no rationalization, the liberal was forced to add a further component of despair.

V

Here then is the remarkable problem of our time. In these strange days we have had an economy which, on grounds of sheer physical performance, few would be inclined to criticize. Even allowing for the conformist tradition in American social thought, the agreement on the quality of the performance of American capitalism is remarkable. The absence of any plausibly enunciated alternative to the present system is equally remarkable. Yet almost no one has felt very secure. The conservative has seen an omnipotent government busy altering capitalism to some new, unspecified, but wholly unpalatable design. Even allowing for the exaggeration which is the common denominator of our political comment and of conservative fears in particular, he apparently has felt the danger to be real and imminent. Under the Democrats we are but one session of Congress or one bill removed from a cold revolution. At most Republicans provide only a temporary and half-hearted interruption in the dash towards disaster. The liberal contemplates with alarm the great corporations which cannot be accommodated to his faith. And, with the conservative, he shares the belief that, whatever the quality of current performance of the economy, it is certain not to last. Yet in the years in question we survived. And many more people were content with the economic system than unhappy.

It can only be, then, that something was wrong with the

current or accepted interpretation of American capitalism. This, indeed, was the case. Conservatives and liberals, both, were the captives of ideas which caused them to view the world with misgivings or alarm. Neither the structure of the economy nor the role of government conformed to the pattern specified, even demanded, by the ideas they held. The American government and the American economy were both behaving in brazen defiance of their rules. If their rules had been binding, they would already have suffered severely. The conservative, who had already had two decades of New and Fair Deals would already have been dispossessed. The liberal, who had already lived his entire life in an economy of vast corporations, would already have been their puppet. Little would have been produced; we should all have been suffering under the exploitation and struggling to pay for the inefficiency of numerous and vast monopolies. The fact that we escaped those misfortunes in these years is a matter of considerable importance. It means that, for the time at least, the trouble lay not with the world but with the ideas by which it was interpreted. It was the ideas which were the source of the insecurity – the insecurity of illusion.

# CHAPTER 2

# The Foundations of the Faith

I

THE late Lord Keynes, in what promises to be one of the more widely quoted passages from his pen, observed that 'the ideas of economists and political philosophers, both when they are right and when they are wrong, are more powerful than is commonly understood. ... Practical men, who believe themselves to be quite exempt from any intellectual influences, are usually the slaves of some defunct economist.' Ideas underlie the uneasiness described in the last chapter. However it would be wrong to suppose they are the sole explanation. Something must also be attributed to mere reaction to change. The well-to-do and the wealthy man will normally be mistrustful of change. This has been so, in the past, in nearly all times and places. It is a simple matter of arithmetic that change *may* be costly to the man who has something; it cannot be so to the man who has nothing. There is always, accordingly, a high correlation between conservatism and personal well-being.

Generalizing more broadly, as the United States proceeds to higher levels of well-being, there is certain to be a steady retreat from social experiment. Indeed, were it not dangerous to extend a trend derived from only one brief decade of prosperity, one could argue that this rejection of social experiment is already far advanced. As this is written, American liberals have made scarcely a new proposal for reform in twenty years. It is not evident that they have had any important new ideas. Reputations for liberalism or radicalism continue to depend almost exclusively on a desire to finish the unfinished social

24

legislation of the New Deal. It was adversity that nurtured this programme; with prosperity social invention came promptly to an end. On domestic matters, liberal organizations have not for years had anything that might be called a programme. Rather they have had a file. Little is ever added. Platform-making consists, in effect, in emptying out the drawers. The Midwest and Great Plains, which once provided Congress with its most disturbing radicals, now returns its staunchest conservatives including also its most determined reactionaries. The political destiny of the United States does not rest with those who seek or who are suspected of wishing to repeal laws, withdraw services, and undo what has been done. This also is change and unwelcomed. But, given peace and prosperity, it no longer rests with those who advocate major social experiment. In a country where well-being is general, the astute politician will be the one who stalwartly promises to defend the *status quo*.*

II

The ideas which are the deeper cause of insecurity are the common heritage of liberals and conservatives alike. These derive from a theory of capitalism which has deeply shaped the

---

* I sense, for example, that the unexpected strength of the Democrats in 1948 lay not with Mr Truman's promise of any great forward steps in economic policy but in his evident willingness to defend what existed including the measures enacted in the New Deal years. The Republican Party, by contrast, was handicapped by the suspicion – which numerous of its spokesmen and supporters reinforced rather than dispelled – that it harboured a deep nostalgia for the past and might seek change in that direction. In 1952, by contrast, General Eisenhower, with rather more capacity to inspire confidence than Mr Dewey, managed to persuade the public that there would be no important backward change.

In the United Kingdom the Conservatives have also capitalized on the defence of the *status quo* and there, as in the United States, ideas on the left have been severely blighted by prosperity.

attitudes of both. This is the system of classical economics which was constructed in the latter part of the eighteenth and during the nineteenth century, primarily in England. Those who would make its acceptance a test of sound Americanism should know that, to a singular degree, it is an alien doctrine. Its principal early architects were Englishmen and Scots. American economists, although they added some important amendments and reproduced it in countless textbooks, contributed comparatively little to the structure itself. Until fairly recent times Americans have not shown high originality in economic theory, and the habit of looking abroad for authority is still strong. It was the classical system, as imported from nineteenth-century England, that became the explicit, and remains the implicit, interpretation of American capitalism.

The bearing of this system on the insecurity stressed in the last chapter becomes evident, even in cursory view, when it is examined in relation to the world it is presumed to interpret. Given this system or, more accurately, an economy constructed to its specifications where there is stout observance of its rules of behaviour, all of the worries of the preceding chapter dissolve. It describes an economic system of high social efficiency – that is to say, one in which all incentives encouraged the employment of men, capital, and natural resources in producing most efficiently what people most wanted. There could be no misuse of private power because no one had power to misuse. An innocuous role was assigned to government because there was little that was useful that a government could do. There was no place in the theory for severe depression or inflation. The system worked. This was the promise, but it was made only to a society with the proper economic institutions and the proper respect for the rules of behaviour which the classical system required. In the contemporary United States few of the preconditions for the system can seriously be supposed to exist. Nor do we pretend to live by its rules. Accordingly, we are forced to assume that we stand constantly in danger of reaping the terrible reward of our neglect and our disobedience. The dangers and even the disasters we risk are no less fearsome because we do not know their precise shape or why they do not come.

### III

The first requirement of the classical system, as everyone is aware, is competition. In the design of the system this was fundamental and, if it was present in a sufficiently rigorous form, it was also enough. In practice, another condition, more properly an assertion, was added in the form of Say's Law of Markets. This held that the act of producing goods provided the purchasing power, neither too much nor too little, for buying them. Thus there was invariable equivalence between the value of what was produced and the purchasing power available to buy that production. It will be evident, even from the most casual reflection, that this comforting doctrine went far to preclude either a serious depression or a violent inflation.

The kind of competition that was necessary for this system was rigorous or, rather, there was a tendency to specify an increasingly rigorous form of competition with the passage of time. The classical economists – Adam Smith, Ricardo, and Mill – were not especially self-conscious in their use of the term. Competition was the rivalry of the merchants of the town or of the cotton manufacturers or pit proprietors of nineteenth-century England. Adam Smith contented himself with distinguishing competition from monopoly by its consequences: 'The price of monopoly is upon every occasion the highest which can be got. ... The price of free competition, on the contrary, is the lowest which can be taken, not upon every occasion indeed, but for any considerable time together.'* But towards the end of the nineteenth century writers began to make explicit what had previously been implied: namely, that competition required that there be a considerable number of sellers in any trade or industry in informed communication with each other. In more recent times this has been crystallized into the notion of many sellers doing business with many buyers. Each is well informed as to the prices at which others are selling and buying – there is a going price of which everyone is aware. Most important of all, no buyer or seller is large enough to control or exercise an appreciable influence on the common price. In the language of the most distinguished modern exponent of the classical system as an economic and political goal, 'The price system will fulfil [its] function only if competition prevails, that is, *if the individual producer has to adapt himself to price changes and cannot control them.*'† The rigour of this definition of competition must be stressed especially to the business reader, for it has been the source of an endless amount of misunderstanding between businessmen and economists. After spending the day contemplating the sales force, advertising agency, engineers, and research men of his rivals the businessman is likely to go home feeling considerably harassed by competition. Yet if it happens that he has measurable control over his prices he obviously falls short of being competitive in the foregoing sense. No one should be surprised if he feels some annoyance towards scholars who appropriate words in common English usage and, for their own purposes, give them what seems to be an inordinately restricted meaning.

Yet the notion of a market for an industry in which no producer or buyer has *any* influence on price is not as improbable

* *Wealth of Nations* (London: P. F. Collier & Sons, 1902 ed.), vol. I, pp. 116–17.

† F. A. Hayek, *The Road to Serfdom* (Chicago: University of Chicago Press, 1944), p. 49. The italics are mine.

as appears at first glance. There is no wheat or cotton grower in the United States whose contribution to the wheat or cotton market is appreciable in relation to the total supply. In January 1949 a Missouri cotton planter made what was believed to be the largest sale of cotton in the history of the Memphis spot market. But the 9400 bales he sold for $1,400,000 was an almost infinitesimal fraction of the 1949 supply. This planter could have gone to heaven with his cotton instead of to Memphis and there would have been no noticeable tremor on any earthly market.

So it is with most other agricultural products. In the nineteenth century, when the classical system was taking form, agriculture contributed a considerably larger share of the national product than at present. Moreover the burgeoning cotton industry, coal-mining, and metal and metal-working industries of England of the day were all shared by numerous producers. The production of each was small in relation to that of all. None could much influence the common price. Finally, in England this was the time of free trade. Sellers were exposed to prices that were made in the markets of the world at large. The kind of competition that was implicit in the pioneering designs of the classical economists of the nineteenth century was not unrealistic. It described a world that then existed; those who formulated the theory did not, as some have since supposed, misjudge reality. They were practical men.

This did not remain the case. Economists, as noted, in seeking to give precision to their language, added rigour to the notion of competition. They also began to require of competition a meaning which would cause it, in turn, to produce the economic and social consequences which earlier economists had associated with it. The definition of competition was gradually accommodated to the requirements of a model economic society; it became not the definition that described reality but the one that produced ideal results. The preoccupation ceased to be with interpreting reality and came to be with building a model economic society. The definition of competition was, in effect, accommodated to the requirements of that model. Its nexus with the competition of the real world, which in turn was in process of change, was no longer maintained.

By the early decades of the present century the task of constructing this model of a capitalist society regulated by competition was virtually complete. It was an intellectual achievement of a high order. As a device, in theory, for ordering the economic relations between men it was very nearly perfect. Socialist theorists – Enrico Barone, the great Italian scholar, and Oskar Lange, the equally notable Polish economist – used the theoretical performance of the competitive model as the goal of a socialist state. Few of the original architects of the competitive model would have defended it as a description of the world as it is – or was. For some the competitive model was a first approximation to reality – it departed from real life only to the extent that there was monopoly in industry or over natural resources, including land, or that government or custom interposed barriers to competition. For others it was the goal towards which capitalism might be expected to move or towards which it might be guided, or a standard by which it might be appraised. For yet others the construction and refinement of the competitive model was a challenging intellectual exercise.

The birth, development, and subsequent career of an idea is something like that of a human. The parents have measurable control over the first two stages but not the third. Once constructed, the competitive model passed into the textbooks and the classrooms. In the absence of any alternative interpretation of economic life, it became the system of virtually all who undertook to teach economics. It was and remains the economics of those who essay to popularize the subject – to instruct in one lesson. The qualifications, and especially the warnings that there had been an abstraction from reality, were lost or neglected. To this day the abstraction, largely undiluted and unqualified, is the principal residuum of the considerable time and expense that goes into the effort to teach economics to Americans.

Man cannot live without an economic theology – without some rationalization of the abstract and seemingly inchoate arrangements which provide him with his livelihood. For this purpose the competitive or classical model had many advantages. It was comprehensive and internally consistent. By asserting that it was a description of reality the conservative could use it as the justification of the existing order. For the reformer it could be a goal, a beacon to mark the path of needed change. Both could be united in the central faith at least so long as nothing happened to strain unduly their capacity for belief.

It is now necessary to examine the performance of the model in more detail.

IV

The notion of efficiency as applied to an economic system is many-sided. It can be viewed merely as a matter of getting the most for the least; this is the commonplace engineering view of efficiency. There is also the problem of getting the particular things that are wanted by the community in the particular amounts in which they are wanted. In addition, if an economy is to be efficient some reasonably full use must be made of the available, or at least of the willing, labour supply. There must be some satisfactory allocation of resources between present and future production – between what is produced for consumption and what is invested in new plant and processes to enlarge future consumption. There must also be appropriate incentive to change; the adoption of new and more efficient methods of production must be encouraged.

Finally – a somewhat different requirement and one that went long unrecognized – there must be adequate provision for the research and technological development which brings new methods and (though one is permitted to deplore them if necessary) new products into existence. All this makes a large bill of requirements.

The peculiar fascination of the competitive model was that, given its particular form of competition – that of many sellers, none of whom was large enough to influence the price – all the requirements for efficiency, with the exception of the very last, were met. No producer – no more than the Kansas wheat grower of fact – could gain additional revenue for himself by raising or otherwise manipulating his price. This opportunity was denied to him by the kind of competition which was assumed, the competition of producers no one of whom was large enough in relation to all to influence the common price. He could gain an advantage only by reducing costs. Were there even a few ambitious men in the business he would have to do so to survive, for if he neglected his opportunities others would seize them. If there are already many in a business it can be assumed that there is no serious bar to others entering it. Given an opportunity for improving efficiency of production, those who seized it, and the imitators they would attract from within and without, would expand production and lower prices. The rest, to survive at these lower prices, would have to conform to the best and most efficient practices. In such a manner a Darwinian struggle for business survival concentrated all energies on the reduction of costs and prices.

In this model, producer effort and consumer wants were also effectively related by the price that no producer and no consumer controlled or influenced. The price that would just compensate some producer for added labour, or justify some other cost, was also the one which it was just worth the while of some consumer to pay for the product in question. Any diminution in consumer desire for the item would be impersonally communicated through lower price to producers. By no longer paying for marginal labour or other productive resources the consumer would free these resources for other employment on more wanted products. Thus energies were also efficiently concentrated on producing what was most desired.

In the competitive model these changes did not raise the threat of unemployment. When the taste of the consumer waned for one product it waxed for another; the higher price for the second product communicated to the producers in that industry the information that they could profitably expand their production and employment. They took in the slack that had been created in the first industry. Even had the consumer decided to save, the saving was for investment – for another kind of expenditure. In any case it was always open to the worker in this system to insure his own employment. Any particular employer was restrained from expanding employment only because the outlay for the added employment was not covered by the resulting increase in income at the going price. The worker seeking employment had it within his own power to alter this delicate balance by offering to work for a lower wage. By doing so he could always make it worth the while of an employer to give him a job. A union, by restraining such wage-cutting, could obviously do damage in this delicately adjusted Elysium. But unions were not a part of the system.

v

There was never full agreement among the architects of the model on the manner in which labour and the other productive resources of the community were allotted as between consumption and investment – between current use and the production of plant, equipment, utilities, and public works which would yield their return only over a period of time in the future. However, despite sectarian disputes on details, there was something close to a consensus on the nature of the underlying process. Here as elsewhere competition rendered efficient service. The competition of those who sought the prospective return from plant machinery, utility, or other investment established a price, in the form of the rate of interest, for those who were willing to save from current consumption and thereby make these investments possible. A high return from additional investment would bid up the price for savings. This would lead to more savings and less current consumption. Resources would thus be freed for investment. By the same process the community's desire for goods for current consumption would be balanced against the prospect of having more and different goods as the result of investment.

If it is assumed that immediate consumption is man's normal preference, and that he will only save if he is paid to do so, it is wholly unnatural to suppose that anyone would first deprive himself of consumer's goods and then, by not turning over his savings for investment, deprive himself also of the reward for his thrift. Accordingly, whether a man consumed or saved, his income was in either case spent. But even the stubborn hoarder – and no one was quite so scorned by the nineteenth-century builders of the competitive model – did no irreparable damage. By getting income and neither spending it nor allowing others to do so, those who hoarded withheld some demand from the market. The only effect of this was that the impersonally determined prices for goods fell as supply exceeded demand. Others then found their current income buying more than before. Their spending offset the additions to the misers' hoards.

Here was the basis of the notion that there could never be an excess of savings – that the aggregate of demand for all goods must always equal their supply. This was Say's Law – the claim upon immortality of Jean Baptiste Say, the French interpreter of Adam Smith. Few ideas have ever gripped the minds of economists so firmly as Say's Law; for well over a hundred years it enjoyed the standing of an article of faith. Whether a man accepted or rejected Say's Law was, until well into the nineteen-thirties, the test of whether he was qualified for the company of reputable scholars or should be dismissed as a monetary crank.

Say's Law reinforced the conclusion that, in the competitive model, there would always be full use of willing labour. As a result, to the extent that the model was taken to be an approximation to reality, no serious consideration could be given to the possibility or fact of a bad depression. A depression must involve some interruption in the flow of spending – some general reduction in demand for goods below the capacity of the economy to supply them. What is being spent at any given time for consumers' goods is obviously being spent. Interruptions between the receipt of income and its ultimate disposal must be sought for in that part of income that is saved. But Say's Law arrested any search for trouble in this area by declaring that savings or their equivalent must also be spent. A decrease in expenditures by consumers would only mean an increase in saving and investment expenditure. Under such circumstances it was impossible to suppose that a general and progressive reduction in spending – without which, as a moment's thought will suggest, there could be no depression – could get under way.

There was some room in this system for rhythmic cycles of good business and bad. So long as the principal effect of such movements was on profits and the rate of economic growth, rather than on employment, no serious collision with Say's Law occurred. And, in fact, the business cycle became the object of a good deal of statistical study, especially in the

United States. Much data could be gathered, and many charts could be drawn without trespassing on Say. But until the mid-thirties, in both England and the United States, the notion of the grave depression was not only foreign to the accepted system of economics but its admission was largely barred to analysis. Unemployment, which was sufficiently a fact so that it could not be ignored, was generally associated with the activities of unions. Unions prevented the worker from getting himself employed by preventing him from reducing the wage at which he offered to work. He was thus restrained from making it worth the while of an employer to hire him. This was not the dogma of mossbacks; it was the only important avenue to an explanation left by Say and the competitive model. As late as 1930, Sir William Beveridge, a modern symbol of progressive ideas, firmly asserted that the effect, at least potentially, 'of high wages policy in causing unemployment is not denied by any competent authority.'*

Say's Law and the resulting sterility of the interpretations of business fluctuations help explain the rather passive role played by economists in the very early years of the Great Depression. Many scholars of reputation either said nothing or vigorously but unhelpfully condemned unbalanced budgets or relief to farmers, businessmen, banks, and the unemployed.†

* He subsequently continued: 'As a matter of theory, the continuance in any country of a substantial volume of unemployment which cannot be explained by specific maladjustments of place, quality, and time is in itself proof that the price being asked for labour as wages is too high for the conditions of the market; demand for and supply of labour are not finding their appropriate price for meeting.' William Beveridge, *Unemployment* (New York: Longmans, Green & Co., 1930), pp. 362–71.

† Especially in the field of monetary policy the initiative passed to men who were not beholden to Say's Law because they had not worked in the main stream of economic theory. This was true, for example, of the late Professor George F. Warren of Cornell, the author of the famous gold-buying policy, and of Messrs Foster and Catchings,

Politics, in all cases, dictated another and more positive course of action – and the judgements of politicians, not of economists, as viewed in retrospect, reflected the course of wisdom. Fortunately the economists were soon to be rehabilitated by the intellectual repeal of Say's Law.

To return to the competitive model. Clearly it either solved the operating problems of the economy, including the great questions of social efficiency, or, as in the case of the severe depression, it excluded the problem from consideration. Efficiency in its various forms was assured by the pressure on the individual firm to produce cheaply and to keep abreast of others in progress, and by the role of an impersonally determined price in passing gains along to consumers and in passing their demands back to producers. The same price structure, abetted by flexible wages and a theory which identified the act of saving with the fact of investment, went far to preclude unemployment. Say's Law canonized the doubtful points. The reader will already be able to understand the depths of the nostalgia for such a mechanism, however rigorous its specifications. It is also possible to understand how the conviction that its requirements were being ignored, or the admission that the model could never be achieved in practice, could leave a community, which had long used this system as a reference point in interpreting its economy, with a sense of profound disquiet.

---

whose work received wide attention at this time. These were also the years when Major Douglas achieved immortality with his revelation on social credit.

# CHAPTER 3

# The Problem of Power

I

ITS solution of the problem of efficiency was what commended the competitive model to the economist. Efficiency has long been a near fetish of economists and, in the beginning, there was a strong humanitarian basis for this preoccupation. Until the nineteenth century, grinding poverty had at all times and in nearly all places been the fate of all but a minority of mankind. For the relief of this poverty, nothing could be quite so important as to get more production from existing manpower and resources. Indeed, in a world where there was little unemployment, no other remedy for poverty was available, given current income distribution and the considerable political discomfort and frustration that have so often been the fortune of those who advocated more equitable distribution of income. The prospect of alleviating poverty, Marshall observed, 'gives to economic studies their chief and their highest interest'.*

For the businessman and the political philosopher, by contrast, the appeal of the competitive model was its solution of the problem of power. This is still the basis of its hold on the American conservative. Indeed, for most Americans free competition, so called, has for long been a political rather than an economic concept.

The role of power in American life is a curious one. The privilege of controlling the actions or of affecting the income and property of other persons is something that no one of us

* Alfred Marshall, *Principles of Economics* (New York: Macmillan Co., 1920, 8th ed.), p. 4.

can profess to seek or admit to possessing. No American ever runs for office because of an avowed desire to govern. He seeks to serve – and then only in response to the insistent pressure of friends or of that anonymous but oddly vocal fauna which inhabit the grass roots. We no longer have public officials, only public servants. The same scrupulous avoidance of the terminology of power characterizes American business. The head of the company is no longer the boss – the term survives only as an amiable form of address – but the leader of the team. It is years since the United States has had a captain of industry; the brass-bound officer who commands has now been entirely replaced by the helmsman who steers. No union leader ever presents himself as anything but a spokesman for the boys.

Despite this convention, which outlaws ostensible pursuit of power and which leads to a constant search for euphemisms to disguise its possession, there is no indication that, as a people, we are averse to power. On the contrary few things are more valued, and more jealously guarded by their possessors, in our society. Prestige in Congress is nicely graded to the number of votes the particular member influences or the potency of his committees. The amount of authority a public servant exercises or – a rough index of this in the lower reaches of the public service – the number of people working under his direction are the accepted measure of his importance in Washington. It is ordinarily taken for granted in the public service that both authority and subordinates will be eagerly accumulated by the energetic man.

Prestige in business is equally associated with power. The income of a businessman is no longer a measure of his achievement; it has become a datum of secondary interest. Business prestige, as a moment's reflection will suggest, is overwhelmingly associated with the size of the concern which the individual heads. Indeed, American business has evolved a system of precedence hardly less rigorous than that of Victorian England

and is based almost exclusively on corporate assets. In the business peerage the ducal honours belong to the heads of General Motors, Standard Oil of New Jersey, Du Pont, and the United States Steel Corporation. The earls, baronets, knights, and squires fall in behind in reasonably strict accordance with the assets of their respective firms. In our time the man who is merely rich is of little consequence. Homage is, to be sure, paid to the 'small but successful' businessman. But the very form of the phrase shows that he has had to surmount the handicap of being small to earn his place in the sun.

The reason is not that the business community pays single-minded obeisance to corporate size and therewith to the men who head the largest concerns. Rather it is that the size of the corporation which the individual heads is again a rough index of the power the individual exercises. With size goes the ultimate responsibility for the decisions affecting the largest number of employees, over prices that affect the largest number of customers, over investment policies which work the greatest change in the income, livelihood, or landscape of the community. While the individual must disavow his interest in making such decisions, his colleagues in the respect they accord him show as clearly as do Congressmen and public servants in their respective fields the direction of their own ambitions.

II

Power obviously presents awkward problems for a community which abhors its existence, disavows its possession, but values its exercise. In the nature of man, the alarm over the exercise of such power runs to its use by second persons. The businessman is not disturbed about the use of authority of which, by hard work and merit, he has become the custodian; he is alarmed about its misuse by government. The liberal naturally views the exercise of private business power with concern. On acquiring public office he is not likely to be persuaded of the danger of misusing his own righteously won authority. This tendency to alarm over the possession of power by other people is greatly enhanced by the convention of denying that one possesses power. The conventional assertion that one has none is readily translated into belief. In any case, the man who is possessed of authority, private or public, is always likely to be more conscious of the checks and reins on his decisions than of his power to reach them. A decision which one is free to make rarely impresses one as an exercise of power. To the extent that it makes any impression at all it is likely to seem a rather obvious exercise of intelligence. A decision on which one is blocked by the authority of another is a very different matter. It is bound to make a deep impression. The impression will also, normally, be one of arbitrary or egregious misuse of power. This is why we live in a world of constant protests against the authority of others and of replies which reflect a deep and usually genuine content of injured innocence.

The competitive model provided an almost perfect solution of the problem of power as aggravated by these conventions and attitudes. Given its rigorous prescription of competition, there was very little scope for the exercise of private economic power and none for its misuse. And with the private exercise of economic power so circumscribed, there was no need for public authority to regulate it. Specifically, if no business is large enough to influence prices on the market in which it sells or on the market in which labour or materials are bought, no one can do anything very harmful to consumers, suppliers, or to the wages of workers because no one has any power over prices charged or prices or wages paid. The man who is moved to exploit his consumers through unduly high prices will survive only long enough to discover that they have deserted him in favour of his numerous competitors who are not exploiting anyone. To pay a worker less than the going wage is to invite him to go where the going wage is paid. It requires only a moment's reflection to conclude that a businessman with power neither to overcharge his customers nor to underpay his labour (and for similar reasons his other suppliers) has very little power to do anybody ill.

To minimize the exercise of private power, and especially the opportunity for its misuse, was to remove most of the justification for exercise of government authority over the economy. It is unnecessary for government to control the exercise of private power if it does not exist in any harmful form. And since the efficiency of the economic system is already at a maximum without government interference, it must be presumed that any intervention of government would reduce efficiency. In a state of bliss, there is no need for a Ministry of Bliss.

### III

In the competitive model, intervention by the state in the economy was excluded with equal rigour whether the motives of the state were assumed to be malevolent or benign. The model was formulated in a day when good intentions by the state and its servants could not be assumed. The most vigorous of the political philosophers associated with its design, Jeremy Bentham, sought for nothing so eagerly as to minimize the role of corrupt public officials. There was good reason for this. Until well into the nineteenth century in England, and well into the present century in most of the rest of the western world, the motives of the state authority, in relation to the economy, were at least episodically rapacious or corrupt. In the United States, until the present century, the federal government was ordinarily the patron, in economic matters, of those best situated for extracting favours and of its own employees.

The doctrine of the malignant state is not quite dead. A modern treatise on the American economy concludes that, through progressive income taxation, the government more or less deliberately 'deprives its successful citizens of their product and gives it to the less successful; thus it penalizes industry, thrift, competence, and efficiency, and subsidizes the idle, spendthrift, incompetent, and inefficient. By despoiling the thrifty it dries up the source of capital, reduces investment and the creation of jobs, slows down industrial progress ...'* Not even the intentions of Jackson could have been viewed more dismally by a Boston merchant. But there can be little doubt that this is a minority view. In the United States, as in the parliamentary democracies in general, the great majority of the people have come to regard the government as essentially benevolent. To the extent that the New Deal in the United States had revolutionary significance the revolution was in attitudes of the great masses of the people towards the federal government. Within the span of a few years a comparatively detached and impersonal mechanism, hitherto identified with tariff-making, tax-collecting, prohibition, Farmers' Bulletins, and the National Parks, came to be regarded as a protector and even as a friend of the people at large and their shield against adversity. The actions of the government might not be considered entirely predictable but there was no doubt that its motives were thought good.

However, the competitive model also excluded power that was exercised in the name of welfare and good intentions. Well intentioned or not, such intervention was at best redundant and worst harmful. This explains why, among those who interpret the world by the competitive model, the epithet 'do-gooder' can be one of greater opprobrium than 'evil-doer'. It also explains their alarm as changing attitudes have swept the state into activities inconsistent with its role in the model.

* *The American Individual Enterprise System. Its Nature, Evolution, and Future.* By The Economic Principles Commission of the National Association of Manufacturers (New York: McGraw-Hill Book Co., Inc., 1946), p. 1019.

IV

For a community that finds power agreeable in the first person and abhorrent in the second, the competitive model gave men of striking differences in viewpoint a strong unity of purpose. All could find within it a programme suited to their temperament and interest. Thus for the businessman it provided a strong justification for resisting the intrusions of government. It also provided an answer to those who suggested that *he* had undue power. Competition denied it to him; his seeming power was a mirage. Better aware than anyone else of the restraints on his decisions, he could believe it. His critics cherished the competitive model because it denied power both to the entrepreneur and to government. They could suspect the businessman of possessing economic power but their remedy was only to have a purer form of the same kind of economy as the businessman himself espoused.

It is scarcely surprising that many men continued to cling to the competitive model as an idea long after its substance had seemingly deserted them.

Nor can it be supposed that faith in a system of ideas which seemed to solve so many problems could disintegrate without important consequences. But it has disintegrated. This has been partly the result of changes in the underlying reality. To a much greater extent it has been the counterpart of the process by which the competitive model was built. What was elaborated in the world of ideas could be destroyed in the world of ideas; what economists gave they could take away. Since it was not the economy so much as the ideas that changed, the consequences, happily, have been less physical than psychological, less of the stomach than of the mind. To the process of disintegration and its consequences I now turn.

# CHAPTER 4

# The Abandonment of the Model

## I

THE system of ideas just outlined – the theory of capitalism and the solution of the problem of power it provided – was vulnerable at two points. In the realm of ideas there was its pivotal dependence on competition, on a definition of competition that had tended to become increasingly precise and hence increasingly brittle. Even the staunchest defenders of the doctrine required a rigorous form of competition – with Professor Hayek they held that it had to be the competition in which 'the individual producer has to adapt himself to price changes and cannot control them.'* There was also, in the world of reality, the need for performance. The system had to work. Were the assumption of competition to be undermined, it would be a devastating blow. So, equally, would be a failure in performance. Both blows fell simultaneously in the decade of the thirties.

The first blow had been in the making for many years – that it would come sooner or later was implicit in the pattern of industrial growth that has occurred both in the United States and throughout the western world. With many notable exceptions – agriculture, the textile and garment industries, soft-coal mining, wholesale and retail trade, shoe manufacturing – the number of firms participating in a business is likely to be at its maximum within a few years or even a few months after the business is born. Thereafter there is, typically, a steady decline until a point of stability is reached with a handful of massive

* See page 28.

survivors and, usually, a fringe of smaller hangers-on. Thenceforward the changes in the industry are in the relative positions of the established firms. This is not a universal pattern of development but it is a typical one. The automobile, steel, rubber, farm implement, tobacco, liquor, chemical, and radio industries all took such a course. So, unless they are exceptions to the rule, will such new industries – as this is written – as the manufacture of television sets and the mining of uranium.

The process by which the typical industry passes from the hands of the many to the few has not been well understood. Not infrequently in the United States it has been identified with a design by someone to acquire monopoly control of enterprise. There have been spectacular searches for the devils. The Muckrakers and the Pujo investigation of 1912 looked for the *deus ex machina* of the consolidation movement of the preceding decades – and thought they found it in the bankers. (These were the years which produced International Harvester, International Nickel, International Paper, International Silver, and International Salt, as well as the more modestly titled United States Steel, all attesting by their names the generous horizons of the men who put them together.) In the thirties the Pecora investigation and the Temporary National Economic Committee looked, somewhat less specifically, for the architects of the utilities combines, the big motion-picture companies, the theatre chains, and the burgeoning chain store systems.

To regard the tendency towards concentration of ownership in an industry as the result of some individual's imperial design is to miss the point. In fact, the causes are deeply organic. Except in industries where the maximum advantages of size are realized at a relatively small volume of production – agriculture, some types of trade, and some few fields of mining and manufacture – entry into an industry is easy only when it is very new. Then the recruitment of capital by all is based on hope and promise and it is impossible to distinguish the promise of an embryo Ford from that of a Preston Tucker, the highly resourceful but already half-forgotten promoter of an exceedingly exiguous auto in the years after the Second World War. No aspirant has the advantage of organization and experience; none has achieved the status of a comparatively sure thing. Since all are beginners all are small, and the capital requirements for any one are modest.

With the growth of the industry the firms already in operation also grow. In doing so they realize whatever technical economies there may be in larger-scale production and the successful ones also acquire, either directly from earnings or from their reputation for making them, the wherewithal in new capital for further growth.

These firms also acquire – a point somewhat neglected by economists – the economies of experience. The development of an industrial enterprise is a fairly intricate task in organization and administration. It can be accomplished easily only when it is accomplished slowly – when there is opportunity to search for talent, to try new men out a few at a time, and when there is leisure to reassign, promote to innocuousness, or detach with regrets the inevitable mistakes. Only a little of this can be afforded at any given time.

The result is a passive but highly effective handicap on the latecomer. In this race the horse with the poorest record, or no record, must carry the greatest weight. Capital must be found in spite of the fact that there are other firms that are a better prospect for the investor. Once the Reconstruction Finance Corporation eased the problem of entry of new firms and it is indeed significant that the new arrivals in such industries as automobile, steel, and aluminium production in recent years have all had capital from this source. But even if the aspirant has or had* the necessary merit and friendships to obtain government funds he must still contend with new foremen and untried supervisors and engineers and he must risk the gaucheries of untried executives. An old firm may have a few neophytes; the new firm has few others. It must accomplish, often in a few months, the tasks of organization which those already in the field have worked out, step by step, over many years. As a result, in an established industry, where the scale of production is considerable, there is no such thing as freedom of entry. On the contrary, time and circumstances combine to bar the effective entry of new firms.

At the same time that entry becomes difficult or impossible, the forces which tend to reduce the number already in the industry continue. Weaklings may still fail, and disappear, especially in more difficult times. Good times make it easy to finance consolidations and tempting for the strong company to expand and the weak to sell out. Thus, both adversity and prosperity work alike to reduce the number of firms in an industry. The combination of a low or zero birthrate and a continuing death rate must, rather unavoidably, be a declining population.

The growth pattern here described is not peculiar to the United States. Industrial development appears to have followed a roughly similar path in other advanced countries. There may, however, be something distinctive about the final equilibrium in the United States. In Western Europe the end

---

* The liquidation of the RFC in the early fifties was a serious blow to competition as it is commonly understood. On the whole, this agency was probably a more effective contributor to freedom of entry than the anti-trust laws. Any important tampering with the latter, it might be noted, would have provoked an enormous outcry from men of good will. The RFC, uncelebrated in the legal and economic folklore of competition, disappeared with scarcely a sound. As so often one finds the American liberal setting greater store by the symbol than by the substance.

result, abetted by cartel agreements, has frequently been a single massive survivor or combination. With us it is far more typically a few large firms together with a fringe of small ones. This equilibrium is apparently associated with a certain equality of strength among the major survivors coupled with a measure of equality of size that makes it difficult for any one large firm to buy another out. At this stage, too, consolidation is consolidation of giants. It has become a sufficiently massive and spectacular affair so that public opinion and the possibility of adverse attention from the Department of Justice both act as deterrents. At the same time the price competition of the large firms is likely to be sufficiently circumscribed by caution so that the smaller fringe can live, albeit often precariously, under the umbrella the large firms provide.

Having reached this stage, little further change occurs in the membership of the typical industry. There is no more cherished view of the American economy than that which regards it as a biological process in which the old and the senile are continually being replaced by the young and vigorous. It is a pleasant but far-fetched fiction. In fact the present generation of Americans, if it survives, will buy its steel, copper, brass, automobiles, tyres, soap, shortening, breakfast food, bacon, cigarettes, whisky, cash registers, and caskets from one or another of the handful of firms that now supply these staples. As a moment's reflection will establish, there hasn't been much change in the firms supplying these products for several decades.

II

An economy where the typical industry is shared by a few firms is awkwardly inconsistent with a theory of capitalism which requires that power to affect prices or wages or output or investment be impersonally governed by the reactions of the many. During the thirties, as the result of a singularly important series of studies, the notion that there was extensive concentration in American industry gained wide acceptance. The first of these studies was the epochal investigation by Adolf A. Berle and Gardiner C. Means into the proportion of national wealth, industrial wealth, and corporate assets owned by the two hundred largest non-financial corporations.* This was followed by further investigations under government auspices by Means,† more yet by the Temporary National Economic Committee, and, since the Second World War, still further studies by the Federal Trade Commission and the Department of Commerce.

Three questions were at issue in these studies, namely: how important are a minority of very, *very* big corporations in the American economy? To what extent are markets divided between a relatively small number of large firms – large, that is, in relation to the markets they share? Does concentration become greater year by year?

There is still something less than complete agreement on the answers and not all of the discussion which these studies have provoked has been of Olympian objectivity. Some have seen in them the support they were seeking for their warnings on monopoly and their belief that the antitrust laws should be more sternly enforced. The critics of the figures have, with a few exceptions, been men who are deeply devoted to the economic and political system identified with the competitive model as an economic and political goal. They have been in the always equivocal position of the man who must testify to the virtue of a well-loved mistress.

Yet the principal conclusions, if stated with reasonable moderation, are not subject to serious challenge and they have,

* *The Modern Corporation and Private Property* (New York: Commerce Clearing House, Inc., 1932; and Macmillan Co., 1932).

† *The Structure of the American Economy. Part I. Basic Characteristics. National Resources Planning Board* (Washington: U.S. Government Printing Office, 1939).

in fact, gained wide acceptance. The importance of the large corporation, and the large proportion of manufacturing, transportation, utilities service, and mining which a comparatively small number perform, is clear. Means calculated* that for 1933 the 200 largest non-financial (i.e., producing or controlling as distinct from financing) corporations and their subsidiaries had approximately fifty-seven per cent of the total assets of all such corporations. A more recent investigation by the Federal Trade Commission estimated, for the year 1947, that the 113 largest manufacturing corporations owned forty-six per cent of the property, plant, and equipment employed in manufacturing.†

Whatever the margin of error in these figures, it cannot be great enough to alter the essential conclusion which is that a small number of large corporations are responsible for a very substantial proportion of all industrial activity. And, in fact, this conclusion is not seriously challenged by serious men.

That the typical industry is shared by a relatively small number of corporations – that there is concentration in individual markets as well as in the economy as a whole – has provided more opportunity for debate. So, also, have the attempts to show that concentration is increasing year by year. With reference to the latter the evidence is, in fact, decidedly frail. It may well be that the appearance of new industries – television, air freight carriage, gambling are notable post-Second World War examples – is sufficient to offset the consolidation that goes on within older industries.

---

* *The Structure of the American Economy*, loc. cit.

† The Federal Trade Commission, *The Concentration of Productive Facilities, 1947* (Washington: U.S. Government Printing Office, 1949). However other types of assets, notably inventories and cash, are also indispensable for operations and there is some evidence from Means's earlier studies that to confine the comparison to physical assets is to maximize the concentration ratio that is shown. (Cf. *Structure of the American Economy*, p. 107.)

The measurement of the concentration within industries has run afoul of the imprecision of the word industry. As this term is used in everyday discourse and as it is used for statistical purposes, it groups together the production of some highly unrelated products and it runs boundaries between products that are closely interchangeable. Willys Jeeps and Cadillacs are both products of the automobile industry, but a cut in price or a doubling of output of Jeeps is not a datum of perceptible importance to the Cadillac Division of General Motors. Copper, brass, and aluminium, which are closely interchangeable for many uses, are products of different industries. At the same time, the notion of an industry as a group of firms supplying roughly the same market has practical usefulness and it would be impossible to get along without it.

In spite of these problems, which have provided an almost unparalleled opportunity for quibbles,* these studies affirm, at least, that over an important sector of the American economy individual markets are shared by a small number of producers. In the production of motor vehicles, agricultural machinery, rubber tyres, cigarettes, aluminium, liquor, meat products, copper, tin containers, and office machinery the largest three firms in 1947 did two thirds or more of all business. In steel, glass, industrial chemicals, and dairy products the largest six accounted for two thirds. There is a similar degree of concentration in a host of less important or derivative industries. And in a number more – gasoline, cement, mixed fertilizer, and milk distribution – markets that are necessarily regional or local are typically divided between a similarly small number of sellers.†

There are numerous industries where the number of firms

---

* For an interesting and competent one, see Clair Wilcox, 'On the Alleged Ubiquity of Oligopoly', *Papers and Proceedings of the American Economic Association*, May 1950, pp. 67ff.

† Federal Trade Commission, op. cit.

serving the same market remains large and where no one or no small number have any considerable proportion of the total business. But for a large and important sector of the economy – indeed for the industries which are commonly supposed to typify American capitalism – this is clearly not the case. On the contrary, as one of the leading contemporary students of market organization has concluded, 'The principal general indications of studies of American market structure are [among others] that concentration of output among relatively few sellers is the dominant pattern.'\* The acceptance of such a conclusion would obviously be damaging to a theory of capitalism based on the notion that markets were shared by many producers no one of them large enough to influence the common prices paid or received.

### III

Meanwhile economic theory, as distinct from economic statistics, had also dealt the competitive model a serious blow. Economists had anciently recognized one major exception to the competition of the many. That was the limiting case of monopoly – the case where one firm was in complete control of all the products of an industry. So long as economists held to this bipolar classification of industries – competition *or* monopoly – the position of competition as a valid assumption concerning the economy was relatively secure. That was because monopoly – the absolute monopoly of the single firm – was so rare as to have the standing only of a curiosity. Apart from the public utilities there was, before the Second World War, only one example that could easily be brought to mind, namely the Aluminium Company of America.† So long as

---

\* Joe S. Bain in *A Survey of Contemporary Economics* (Philadelphia: Blakiston Co., 1948), p. 136.

† Which now, of course, shares the ingot market with the wartime arrivals.

monopoly was so exceptional, competition must be the rule. The economy as a whole must be competitive.

In 1932–3, under the combined attack of an American and a British economist (Professor E. H. Chamberlin of Harvard University* and Mrs Joan Robinson of Cambridge University†) the old bipolar classification of markets, competition *or* monopoly, was abandoned. New categories of markets, neither purely competitive nor fully monopolized, were recognized between the two. In this intermediate zone were industries whose markets had the characteristics of both competition and monopoly. They were monopolistically or imperfectly competitive.

The establishment of a multiple, rather than a double-classification of markets was the most far-reaching contribution of the new theory. It meant, although it wasn't wholly foreseen at the time, the end of the faith in competition in the old sense. Now there were alternatives to the implausible assumption of competition without going to the implausible case of monopoly. The competition of many sellers – the competition of the model – like the control of a market by one, soon came itself to be regarded as an extreme or limiting case. From the statistical investigations as well as from everyday observation it was evident, moreover, that one of the intermediate types of markets – that of few sellers or oligopoly as it came to be called – was of commanding importance. No sooner had oligopoly been recognized as something different from either competition or monopoly than it was on its way to replace competition as the principal assumption by which the industrial economy was interpreted.

* *The Theory of Monopolistic Competition* (Cambridge: Harvard University Press, 1932).

† *The Economics of Imperfect Competition* (London: Macmillan Co., 1933). There are differences of theoretical interest and importance between Professor Chamberlin's and Mrs Robinson's argument which, however, do not bear on the practical consequences which are of concern here.

However, a vast distance separates oligopoly from the competition of the competitive model. Price-making in markets where there are a few sellers is not only measurably influenced by the actions of any individual firm but the individual must take into consideration the response of others to his initiative. If he correctly appraises what is advantageous for the industry as a whole, the others presumably will follow his lead. Otherwise they will not. When each seller considers the advantage of any action from the viewpoint of the profits of the industry as a whole he is obviously thinking much as would a monopolist. To assume that oligopoly was general in the economy was to assume that power akin to that of a monopolist was exercised in many, perhaps even a majority, of markets.

In actual practice things are both simpler and more complicated. They are simpler because in most industries where there are few sellers there soon develops a tacit understanding which allows one arm to assume some measure of leadership. This firm makes an appraisal of the price policy that is appropriate for itself with greater or less consideration of what will be acceptable to the other members of the industry. The others follow its lead. Things are more complicated because, except under conditions of very strong demand, any firm in an industry can initiate price reductions. This normally forces others to follow suit. There is no similar compulsion to follow a price increase. Any one of the large cigarette companies can bring down cigarette prices by lowering its own price. It cannot as certainly bring the others up by raising its prices. As compared with monopoly, one of the mitigating facts about oligopoly is the commanding position of the firm which sees the greatest advantage in low prices.

Price-making under oligopoly is further complicated by the fact that there is never complete substitutability between the products of different sellers. A Ford differs from a Chevrolet and the differences are energetically magnified by the advertising of the companies. This gives to Ford and General Motors some small measure of independence in their prices. The same is true, though in lesser degree, even of chemically identical products like steel or sulphur. Habit, corporate personality, terms, and promptness of delivery will hold customers even in face of minor price differentials.* However, these are details. The important thing is that the doctrines of a monopolistic or imperfect competition paved the way for a destruction of the old assumption of competition on which the competitive model was erected. It is now time to see what took its place.

IV

It is a measure of the magnitude of the disaster to the old system that when oligopoly or crypto-monopoly is assumed it no longer follows that any of the old goals of social efficiency are realized. The producer now has measurable control over his prices. Hence prices are no longer an impersonal force selecting the efficient man, forcing him to adopt the most efficient mode and scale of operations and driving out the inefficient and incompetent. One can as well suppose that prices will be an umbrella which efficient and incompetent producers alike will tacitly agree to hold at a safe level over their heads and under which all will live comfortably, profitably, and inefficiently. There is no longer, by the old line of arguments, any certainty of technical advance. When there are many producers in an industry, some one of them will certainly seize upon any known innovation. In so doing, this pioneer forces

* Economists have commonly worked with a category of markets described as 'undifferentiated' or 'pure' oligopoly. In principle, as in fact, no such category exists and it should be abandoned. If the number of sellers is small they will always be identified as distinct personalities to the buyer. And although their products may be identical, their personalities will not and cannot be. There is always, accordingly, a degree of product differentiation.

others to follow. To resist progress is to perish. If there is only a handful of producers, there is a chance that none will assume the initiative. There is at least the possibility that all will prefer and concur in choosing profitable and comfortable stagnation.

When sellers have gained authority over prices, prices no longer reflect the ebb and flow of consumer demand. It was such price movements in the competitive model which equated consumer desires – as evidenced by their willingness to pay – with what producers found it worth while to supply. When prices are tacitly administered by a few large firms they no longer move freely and production no longer responds automatically to price changes. An increase in demand may bring increased production at the old prices; it may just as well lead to a decision to increase prices and profits with production remaining as before.

In any case it must be assumed that prices will be set and production will be managed, however imperfectly, with an eye to the profits of the industry. One of the oldest conclusions of economics is that a price so set – a monopoly price – must be higher and the resulting output smaller than under conditions of competition. Thus not only does oligopoly lead away from the world of competition, with its promise of efficiency, but it leads towards the world of monopoly. This, anciently, had been viewed as the very antithesis of social efficiency.

There were other bitter consequences of the new assumptions. A close examination of oligopoly shows that price competition, the very motor of the competitive model, is not only sharply circumscribed but has to be. When there are only a few firms in an industry and their products are closely substitutable, a price cut by one company must, as just noted, be matched by the others. Otherwise the firm with the lower price will draw a disproportionate share of the business in the short run and, through operation of habit and customer goodwill, may well retain it in the long run. This the other firms must prevent. An aggressive and persistent price cutter can, accordingly, affect the level of prices and return of the entire industry. Should he persist and provoke retributive action, the ensuing price warfare can be ruinous to all. There is no point set by cost or any other consideration below which prices cannot go. Cuts must be matched and, if the game is fully played through, all can be ruined.

No similar problem arises with the competitive model. No seller can affect prices; none, obviously, can engage in cutthroat price cuttings. There, should prices fall to the level of costs, some firms would withdraw and others curtail output. The resulting reduction in supply would stabilize or raise prices. Costs are a floor below which prices cannot go, at least for very long.

Businessmen who live in the shadow of disastrous price cutting, as do all who share markets with a few firms, protect themselves by a convention. This convention simply outlaws the use of prices as a weapon of competitive warfare. The convention against price competition, when there are only a few sellers in a market, is a matter of great importance. It is also so much a part of customary business practice that where it is well observed its very existence is often unnoticed even by those who adhere to it. Prices continue to change, and they may be changed, at the instance of an aggressive and efficient leader, when that firm knows that the result will be uncomfortable for other firms. But this is very different from using prices as a sanguinary weapon for invading another's markets or separating him from his customers. This the convention prohibits and there is nothing more frightening, in industries where the convention is not rigidly observed, than the news that a price war has broken out. Quite typically the individual who resorts to price competition does so surreptitiously and the opprobrious character of his action is suggested by the terms in which he is normally described: he is irresponsible, a chiseller, an unfair competitor, a man who is guilty of unsound or even un-American business practices. The primitive defender of the convention against price competition finds racial epithets one of the most satisfying ways of assailing the unorthodox competitor.

Nevertheless, a convention against price competition is inevitable under oligopoly. The alternative is self-destruction, which cannot be expected of men with a normal desire to remain solvent and which in any case would serve no useful purpose. Although the market of small numbers clearly precludes aggressive price competition – the uninhibited price movements which the competitive model requires – economists have been very reluctant to concede the fact. They have regularly rebuked the businessman who foreswears price competition as a traitor to the price system. The businessman has been understandably mystified by these attacks. Evidently the test of his faith in competition is his willingness to court disaster in its name.

The final embarrassment from the unravelling of the new ideas was that as price competition in its pristine form disappeared, other forms of competitive behaviour became suspect. The convention against retributive price competition in the market shared by a few large firms does not extend to other forms of commercial rivalry. Individual firms retain their desire to keep and even to enlarge their share of the market. The first is important for survival, the second for both profits and prestige. With price competition ruled out, competitive energies are normally concentrated on persuasion and, especially in consumers' goods, on salesmanship and advertising. The cigarette manufacturer recruits customers, not by the self-defeating and dangerous device of cutting cigarette prices but, with the unreluctant aid of his advertising agency, by recourse to the radio, billboards, and television screens and through magazines and the press. This is competition but no longer the kind of competition that is eligible for the liberal's defence. On the contrary, the very instrument which once rewarded the community with lower prices and greater efficiency now turns up assailing its ear with rhymed commercials and soap opera and rendering the countryside hideous with commercial art. Competition becomes an exercise in uniquely ostentatious waste. What hath Adam Smith wrought?

In any case no one could any longer argue very seriously that the cost and volume of even the comparatively inoffensive forms of competitive selling and advertising were in response to popular demand. Not only had the old pressure for efficiency in production been lost, but now there was a positive premium on expenditures on distribution. This was all readily assimilated to the new theory. Indeed, given the market of the few it was normal and natural.

One consequence of the new ideas was to place economic theory sharply in opposition to the burgeoning advertising industry. Not unnaturally, those advertising men who take their profession seriously, and have the normal human wish to be wanted, have not found it pleasant to be considered extraneous. Since they were hardly in a position to devise a new system of theory which would re-establish their place in the scheme of things, they have been reduced to stating, often with some vigour, that it is advertising that made this country what it is today. The adman was one of the many displaced persons who was caught up in the retreat from the competitive model.

v

Such was the general state of ideas on economic efficiency in the main tradition of economics – in the impeccable line of descent from Adam Smith, David Ricardo, and Alfred Marshall – by roughly the beginning of the Second World War. By evolution, from a system where nearly everything worked out for the best, economists found themselves with a system where nearly everything seemed to work out for the worst.

It would be a mistake to exaggerate the alarm with which the generality of economists viewed this result. One author did go so far as to plead with his colleagues 'to recognize that the concept of a system of monopoly is self-contradictory and the very negation of everything economics stands for'.* They were adjured to see no evil. In a great personal tragedy, Heinrich von Stackelberg, a brilliant German contributor to the new theory, apparently lost all hope of any order in the economy except as might be provided by the state. Almost alone among the German economists of any distinction he became for a period an active National Socialist.

A certain number of economists have also undertaken to revive the faith of their colleagues in the existence, actual or potential, of the competition of the competitive model. One of the lesser literary flowerings in the years after the Second World War was a series of books and articles celebrating the virtues, even the magic, of the uninhibited price system. But even this task was assumed, in the main, by popular writers whose faith in pure competition had not been weakened by contact with the new ideas.

This philosophical detachment of the economists is to be explained in part by their much greater interest ever since the thirties in the problem of depression and by their preoccupation with factors bearing more directly on the total performance of the economy. None the less, the new market theory had a profound effect. A generation ago American economists, an inconvenient bias towards free trade apart, were counted among the staunchest allies of the businessman and among the nation's most notable defenders of the *status quo*. Partly as the

* Eduard Heimann, *History of Economic Doctrines* (New York: Oxford University Press, 1945), p. 219.

result of the new ideas, they have since acquired an almost un-excelled reputation for waspishness. The very term economics has come to be identified in the minds of many conservatives, if not with radicalism, at least with an inordinate capacity to find fault. This, no doubt, was a healthy change. Economists should never be popular; men who afflict the comfortable serve equally with those who comfort the afflicted and one cannot suppose that American capitalism would long prosper without the critics its leaders find such a profound source of annoyance. However, the new ideas had the far-reaching consequence of bringing into question a basic supposition of capitalism – the supposition that it was socially efficient. Here is the first of the causes of insecurity which it is the task of this essay to isolate.

# CHAPTER 5

# The Ogre of Economic Power

I

THE old solution of the problem of economic power suffered the same devastation from the new measures of market concentration and the new ideas as did the old confidence that social efficiency would be maximized. The competition of the competitive model solved the problem of private economic power by denying it, at least in a dangerous form, to anyone. The exception was the rare case of the monopolist. He did have plenary authority over his prices and production and therefore over the wealth and welfare of some part of the community. It was agreed by everyone, the monopolists themselves excepted, that such power was evil and that it should be struck down or be made subject to regulation by the state wherever it was found. The regulation of monopoly represented one of the few instances where, given the competitive model, it was agreed that the state would have to exercise its authority in the economy.

If there are only a handful of firms in the typical industry, and if they recognize their interdependence, as they must both for profit and for survival, then privately exercised economic power is less the exception than the rule in the economy. It is also of a piece with the power anciently associated with monopoly. This was the clear conclusion of the new ideas. And the fact of such power, once identified by the theory, could readily be verified by observation. The executives of the United States Steel Corporation, the longtime price leaders in the steel industry, do have authority to raise and lower the prices they charge for their own steel. When they exercise that power the rest of the industry normally follows. The same executives make decisions on where to build new plants and how much plant to build, what to pay in dividends and, subject to a periodic trial of strength with the union, what wages to pay. They have latitude on all of these matters; they are not the automatons of market forces. These decisions also affect the wealth and income of hundreds of thousands of people. As with steel so with the great core of American industry. The new theory suggested the existence of such power; the eye confirmed it.

Nothing could be more disturbing, in light of long-standing attitudes towards private economic power and the inflammatory connotation long given to the term monopoly, than the realization that economic power belonging to the *genus* monopoly was commonplace in the economy. Yet such power was now brought nakedly into view. Its existence was affirmed by the statistics and its nature was identified by the theory. No one, neither economist nor businessman, liberal nor conservative, knew quite what to do about this flauntingly indecent exposure.

II

In the American liberal tradition, a finding that private economic power exists has been tantamount to a demand that it be suppressed. As long as economic power was associated with monopoly in the old sense, the liberal had a ready-made formula. He could demand prosecution of the offending monopoly under the Sherman Anti-Trust Act with a view to its dismemberment or, if this latter were impractical as in the case of the utilities, he could advocate public regulation or public ownership. So long as monopoly was considered an exception in a world of competition – a small tumour in a mass of healthy tissue – this was a reasonably practical programme. The number of targets inviting attack was not too great; a vigilant government could be expected to police competition and keep it free.

The notion that there are aspects of monopoly in a large proportion of American industries was bound to bring a major change in liberal attitudes. In fact, it dealt the ancient liberal formula a far more serious blow than has even yet been realized. It is possible to prosecute a few evil-doers; it is evidently not so practical to indict a whole economy. So, where there had once been reasonable agreement among liberals that the antitrust laws were the heart of their programme, something like a three-way split appeared. There were those who did conclude, without too much reflection on the task they were setting for themselves, that the weapons for attacking monopoly would also serve against oligopoly. There were others who concluded that some form of government regulation, generally rather ill defined, would have to assume a task which the antitrust laws could no longer perform. Still others looked at the competition of the giants to see if they could not find something, however removed from the competition of the model, which could still be deemed 'workable'. The common feature of all three enterprises has been a very large component of frustration.

The first reaction, in point of time, was to urge more vigorous enforcement of the antitrust laws against the newly recognized and now ubiquitous monopoly power. As the significance of the new statistics on industrial concentration came to be appreciated in Washington in the late thirties, there was a sharp increase in interest in antitrust enforcement. Thurman Arnold, who was to become the most energetic and successful trust-prosecutor the country has had, was brought to that post in 1938. Appropriations of the Antitrust Division of the Department of Justice under his leadership were increased from $435,000 in 1936 to $1,325,000 in 1941. (They later increased several-fold more.) One of Arnold's cases, that against the large tobacco companies finally decided by the Supreme Court in 1946, also appeared to give a handle for dealing with oligopoly. There was no proof that these firms had entered into any overt agreement on prices. This had been the old test of guilt. Rather, each had merely behaved as though it fully understood and respected the welfare of the group. The leadership of one of their number had been accepted when it was evident that a price decrease would be to the profit of all, and again when it was evident that a price increase would be to the common benefit. Their conviction for such behaviour, the commonplace behaviour of firms when the industry is shared by a few giants, was upheld.* This was an indication that the old weapon against monopoly could be brought to bear on oligopoly.†

However, as more sober consideration was fairly certain to suggest, the effect of the new ideas, by making monopoly diffused and commonplace rather than specific and exceptional, was eventually to weaken the faith in the old liberal programme. Even a successful prosecution, unless it results in a complete breakup of existing firms, does not alter the fundamental behaviour patterns of the industry. So long as there are only a few massive firms in an industry, each must act with a view to the welfare of all. They cannot, by force of law, be made to act as though they had no economic power – as though each were insignificantly small. The leading student of the industry has

* It was not completely commonplace, for the common reduction in price, which occurred in 1933, came at a time when the ten cent or economy brands were making deep inroads into the sales of the majors. Prices were advanced in 1934 when this threat had receded. This timing undoubtedly impressed the courts. *American Tobacco Co. v. United States.* 328 U.S. 781 (1946).

† For an exuberant but competent expression of the optimism with which this case was greeted see Eugene V. Rostow, *A National Policy for the Oil Industry* (New Haven: Yale University Press, 1948), pp. 123ff.

observed that the big tobacco companies, after they had been prosecuted (and rather modestly fined), continued 'to follow essentially the same ... price policies ... they followed before'.* Not long after the prosecution was concluded, this was the subject of bitter complaint before, and by, a Congressional committee.†

As noted, for Chesterfields, Lucky Strikes, and Camels to be in active price competition would be highly inconsistent with the theory by which the market for this product is interpreted. The theory suggests that when the price of one brand changes all must change, or the leader must rescind his move. And the theory correctly interprets the case. Not only is this what has happened but it is the only thing that can happen. Each firm has to consider its actions in light of the responses of the other two. There cannot at the same time be independence and interdependence, and interdependence is the nature of things. As a practical matter in the tobacco business the letter of legality could apparently be met by the companies by maintaining small differences in the wholesale price of cigarettes – differences too small to be reflected to the consumer or to make much difference in the margin of the retailer.‡ Not a great deal else has been changed by the case against the companies, and will not be so long as three companies have a commanding position in the market.

The tobacco companies and industries characterized by oligopoly in general could possibly be dispersed into many small units. But American courts have been notably cautious in the remedies they have invoked under antitrust laws. Decrees dissolving existing companies or forcing them to divest themselves of subsidiaries have been exceedingly and increasingly

* William H. Nicholls, 'The Tobacco Case of 1946', *Papers and Proceedings of the American Economic Association*, May 1949, p. 289.

† 'Monopolistic and Unfair Trade Practices', House Report 2465, 80th Congress, 2nd Session, December 1948, p. 11.

‡ Nicholls, op. cit.

rare. The order divorcing the manufacture of railroad equipment from Pullman car operation has been one of the few of its kind in the past twenty years. However great revolutions are brought about, it is not by litigation.

Thus, while the liberal could hope that the occasional monopoly might be broken up he can scarcely suppose that the antitrust laws are an effective instrument for dispersing the economic power implicit in oligopoly. To suppose that there are grounds for antitrust prosecution wherever three, four, or a half dozen firms dominate a market is to suppose that the very fabric of American capitalism is illegal. This is a notion which can seem sensible only to the briefless lawyer. Yet, to repeat, the interpretation of this market leads relentlessly to the conclusion that the power exercised by a few large firms is different only in degree and precision of its exercise from that of the single-firm monopoly. And clearly it is a lot more important. The liberal, who still searches for old-fashioned monopoly in the modern economy, has been made to feel that his is a search for poison ivy in a field of poison oak.

The evident alternative to competition is public regulation or planning. This has long been supposed to be the only alternative. Under the pressure of the new ideas some American liberals turned consciously to this alternative. 'Striving after individual competition as a neat self-regulating device is fruitless because, by its nature, it cannot be established and maintained by law. We are compelled to pass beyond to the direct selection of economic objectives as a basis for the policy of the state.'* In more cases dissatisfaction with the old formula produced merely a general bias in favour of state intervention in the economy. This goes far to explain why the American liberal, to the endlessly articulated surprise of political

* Arthur R. Burns, *The Decline of Competition* (New York: McGraw-Hill Book Co., Inc., 1936), p. 529.

philosophers, has so often turned up as an advocate of government control.

In fact, the pursuit of this alternative has not been carried very far. It has been carried much less far than conservatives, in their worst dreams, have been inclined to imagine. The most plausible alternative to competition is full public ownership of those industries where competition is ineffective. Few American liberals have even contemplated this possibility and some would indeed be worried were they forced to do so. Few of the halfway houses of control have even been investigated and it is a fair guess that they wouldn't be approved if they were. A minimum requirement of planning, for an economy where competition is no longer assumed to regulate prices, would be systematic price regulation by the state. Few contemporary liberals would find this palatable. The same would be true of anything more and there can't be much that is less.

The truth is that much of the American liberal's modern advocacy of state intervention and planning has been general and verbal. It was a massive deployment of words which concealed, more or less successfully, the fact that he was a man who didn't quite know where he wanted to go. This was illustrated with almost classic finality immediately before the Second World War by the history of the Temporary National Economic Committee – the T. N. E. C. or Monopoly Committee. This Committee was established, in a mood of excitement and even of dedication, in response to the new knowledge of the extent of industrial concentration. In calling for the investigation, President Roosevelt declared: 'The power of a few to manage the economic life of the Nation must be diffused among the many or be transferred to the public and its democratically responsible government. If prices are to be managed and administered, if the Nation's business is to be allotted by plan and not by competition, that power should not be vested in any private group. ....'* The authorizing resolution called for 'a full and complete study and investigation [of] the concentration of economic power in, and financial control over, production and distribution of goods and services'. In the three years of its existence the Committee filled a record of 17,000 pages and produced numerous (and by no means unuseful) reports and monographs. In its conclusions it affirmed that American industry was very concentrated indeed. But it produced no recommendations of any consequence whatever. In one of the most bromidic apologias of modern times, it declared in its final document: 'The members of the committee are not rash enough to believe that they can lay down a programme which will solve the great problems that beset the world, but they are convinced that the information which this committee has assembled ... will enable the people of America to know what must be done if human freedom is to be preserved.'† The Committee was unable to approve of the economy it found but, equally, it was unable to embrace any alternative. It abandoned its task in a miasma of words. Other liberals have had resort to the same escape.

There remains the possibility that within the structure of the market shared by a few firms there are practical restraints on economic power – that there is an attenuated but still workable competition which minimizes the scope for exercise of private market power and which frequently makes this structure preferable to any available alternative. This line of argument has emphasized results. A market is workably competitive if, among other things, there is 'a progressive technology, the passing on to consumers of the results of this progressiveness in

* Message of 29 April 1938. Quoted in *Monopoly and Free Enterprise* by George W. Stocking and Myron W. Watkins (New York: The Twentieth Century Fund, 1951), p. 52.

† *Final Report and Recommendations*. T.N.E.C. Document 35 (Washington: U.S. Government Printing Office, 1941).

the form of lower prices, larger output, improved prices. . . .'*

This pragmatic concern with results is healthy; it has usefully tempered the pessimism which followed in the wake of the new market theory. The notion of workable competition takes cognizance of the sadly overlooked point that over-all consequences, which in theory are deplorable, are often in real life quite agreeable. The difficulty with the notion is that its authors have failed to make clear why what is unworkable in principle becomes workable in practice. This failure, as I shall show presently, lies in the preoccupation with competition. In the competitive model the restraint on the power of any producer was provided by the competition of other producers – it came from the same side of the market. The tendency of any seller to exploit his customers was checked, not by the customers, but by another seller across the street and by many others in the same market. It was natural that in looking for restraints on the behaviour of the large seller, who was one among a few in the market, the search would be made in the same place. Competition, even though it might be different in kind from that of the competitive model, was still the object of the search. Indeed it was assumed that competition was the only possible restraint on private market power. This preoccupation with competition kept the investigators from seeing the actual restraints on market power – restraints that made not competition but the economy workable. These will come in for major considerations a few chapters hence.

---

* Edward S. Mason in 'The Antitrust Laws: A Symposium', ed. by Dexter M. Keezer, *American Economic Review*, June 1949, p. 713. Professor Mason is the leading exponent of the idea of a workable competition. The notion itself owes much to the originality of Professor J. M. Clark ('Toward a Concept of Workable Competition', *American Economic Review*, June 1940).

### III

At first glance the position of the businessman – the head of the large corporation in particular – would appear to have been considerably strengthened by the new shape which the problem of market power had taken. Even though the businessman's market power had come into full view, those who were alarmed were hopelessly divided. Some, accepting the logic of their own analysis, sought a reform of the whole structure of modern corporate enterprise – its disintegration into many small units. This could almost certainly come to nothing. Others were disposed to talk (or muse) about public regulation which they did not define and at which they would almost certainly be alarmed if they did. Others said the situation was workable in some general way. Meanwhile the businessman could remain undisturbed. He could continue to exercise a measure of power in the economy which, given our attitudes towards such authority however fulsomely they are disavowed, cannot be supposed to be unpleasant.

In his more philosophical moods, the businessman might even take a benign view of those who were moved to advocate stronger enforcement of the antitrust laws. Without doubt these laws have performed a notable role in American life as a kind of lightning rod for dissent. Whenever he feels dissatisfied with things as they are, or whenever he is stuck for a programme to deal with something he believes to be wrong, the American radical, it has been said, has an unfailing formula. That is to demand that the antitrust laws be more rigorously enforced. For many they have had the standing of a universal cure: they have even been solemnly invoked as a device for keeping down prices and preventing inflation. No fundamental change in the American economy could or is likely to result from these demands for antitrust enforcement. Thus the businessman has no reason to be alarmed, while the liberal dissident can feel that he has offered a bold and stalwart programme. Had the antitrust laws not been available, and had dissent, accordingly, taken other forms in the past, or were it to do so in the future, the challenge to business power might be formidable.

In practice, matters are a good deal more complicated. The head of the large corporation cannot concede that either he or his firm are possessors of any significant economic power. This is partly a matter of ritual. The competitive model made the firm and its head the automatons of market forces; it is natural that all should recite the familiar defence. Moreover, any admission by the businessman himself that he has substantial economic power is certain to have uncomfortable consequences. Given the conviction that no man has the right to any control over the prices, wages, wealth, or income of a fellow citizen, to admit possession of power is to concede guilt. For any one businessman to make such a concession is to invite the attention of the public and perhaps of the Department of Justice to his firm as a special case.

The head of the large corporation cannot even argue, as he might with logic, that he exercises authority not from choice but from necessity – that, given his size and share of the market, he cannot divest himself at will of responsibility. So to argue is to concede the justifiability of some sort of public regulation or review of his stewardship. It does not help to assert that he uses his power wisely; this is also a concession that the public interest is paramount. The businessman cannot claim that he is the natural arbiter and protector of that interest. Historians have had much sport with the immortal declaration of George F. Baer of the Reading Railroad in 1902 that 'the rights and interests of the labouring man will be protected and cared for ... by the Christian men to whom God in His infinite wisdom has given the control of the property interests of the country. . . .' Wiser men since have found the classical defence, namely, that they are but cogs in a system that accords them no power, to be less dramatic but far safer.

Yet the new ideas contradict flatly the businessman's disavowal of his power. And the ideas are confirmed by everyday decisions of the businessman which are in conflict with his old defence. Having explained that he is governed by the market, the businessman must then decide for or against an increase in the price of steel, whether to proceed with a new mill in New England or on the Delaware and whether to stand or surrender on the question of pay increases and pensions or a guaranteed annual wage. These decisions are important to the income and welfare of many; they cannot be concealed from a community that has come to look for them.

The businessman's disavowal of power also leaves him in an ambiguous position in relation to the same antitrust laws. He cannot deny the utter consistency of these laws with the doctrine by which he defends himself. Competition theoretically prevents him from exercising any important market power and permits him to have the power he has. It is obvious that he cannot oppose measures designed to enforce and strengthen competition.

But the power he does wield – the decisions he does and must take – make him vulnerable to prosecution under the antitrust laws. He must think of the effect of his actions on the industry as a whole, which is how a monopolist thinks. This can easily carry him, by his own acts or those of subordinates, beyond the law. As the antitrust laws are now financed and enforced, the head of any large American corporation must count on the possibility of being hailed into court at least once in his lifetime. There he will face the abhorrent charge of having broken the very rules by which he defends himself and the system. He will stand exposed as a traitor to the basic doctrines of American capitalism. This is not pleasant. Virtually his only defence to the public is that the Department of Justice has made another nasty mistake. A careful reader of corporation reports will learn how frequently this contention must be employed. Especially when the Executive is in the hands of Republicans this plea has a hollow ring. Far more than the penalties or the costs of litigation, these ambiguities of the businessman's position explain why antitrust prosecution has its peculiar standing as a nightmare. This is not another invitation to tears for the hapless free enterpriser. In our society he is paid to worry. A businessman without troubles would not be earning his salary. None the less, like the liberal, the businessman could do with a new and more plausible rationalization of economic power.

# CHAPTER 6

# The Depression Psychosis

I

THE problems of the American economy and polity just discussed have been mostly in the realm of ideas. They would have been a cause of uncertainty and insecurity even had they drawn little reinforcement from everyday experience. But to be a considerable source of alarm they needed the catalysis of experience – an experience which would force a large number of individual citizens to question the efficacy and stability of American capitalism. That experience, in a highly compelling form, was provided by the Great Depression.

The competitive model of a capitalist economy allowed, as noted, for rhythmic increases and decreases in prices and production and even for occasional bouts of unemployment. It did not contemplate the possibility of a catastrophic and enduring depression. Economists, and through them politicians, businessmen, and the public, were insulated from the need to think of such a tragedy by the benign theorem that the act of production provided the purchasing power for all that was produced at approximate full employment.

In 1930 a *really* serious depression was not part of the experience of the current generation of Americans. In late 1920 and early 1921 there was a sharp fall in prices and incomes, and, in somewhat lesser degree, in employment. But the recovery was prompt. Moreover, the whole episode was inextricably associated with the war and its aftermath and could be blamed on what economists are pleased to call exogenous forces. Except by farmers, who continued to feel themselves at a disadvantage, it was almost universally dismissed as the inevitable reaction to the wartime inflation in prices and profits. For an earlier slump of comparable importance it was necessary to go back to the preceding century.

One can only suppose that in 1929 the fates undertook after great deliberation, to shake the confidence of the people of the United States in their economy. Nothing could have been more ingeniously or more elaborately designed to achieve this result. There was the shock effect – the sudden dramatic collapse in stock-market values with which the lives and fortunes of thousands of innocents, who only then became aware of their innocence, had become entwined. This was followed by the inexorable decline in output, values, and employment which, in a little more than two years, cut the value of national production almost in half and left twelve million workers – ten and a half million more than in 1929 – without jobs and mostly without reliable means of support. Those who still had jobs lived in the penetrating fear that their turn would be next. Meanwhile hundreds of thousands of well-to-do citizens either made a sudden and irretrievable descent into poverty or dwelt in the cold fear that they soon would. It would have added to the security of the country if businessmen and bankers had escaped the débâcle. But their well-publicized plight suggested, all too plainly, that they too had no formula for contending with capitalism when the latter was on shipwreck tack. The broken banker was as commonplace a figure in the news as the unemployed worker, and a much less reassuring one. The economy was the impartial destroyer of all.

When there was nothing else to hope for, it could still be hoped that the depression would be temporary. A rhythm of good times and bad was the minimum promise of the competitive model. To this shaky standard the defenders of the system repaired in droves. Then, the most malicious act of all, the depression was made to last ten years. The very notion that depressions in the United States were self-correcting – that there were corners that would be turned – became a national jest. As if to sharpen the point, a modest recovery prior to the summer of 1937, which however had left between seven and eight million still unemployed, was followed by a slump in production that was even sharper than the one following 1929. The Great Depression of the thirties never came to an end. It merely disappeared in the great mobilization of the forties. For a whole generation it became the normal aspect of peacetime life in the United States – the thing to be both feared and expected.

Measured by its continuing imprint on actions and attitudes, the depression clearly stands with the Civil War as one of the two most important events in American history since the Revolution. For the great majority of Americans the Second World War, by contrast, was an almost casual and pleasant experience. Several million found jobs who had doubted whether they might ever find jobs again. Hundreds of thousands of others escaped the routines of middle-class employments, their boredom with which they had concealed even from themselves. Men and women who had never supposed that society would entrust them with responsibility found themselves discharging important tasks with a competence of which they alone had been previously aware. Only a minority experienced the nagging homesickness, the fear, the physical suffering and the mutilation and death which is the less pleasant destiny of the fighting soldier in wartime. Because they were a minority the war left no lasting imprint. The depression which afflicted a great majority of the people did.

The depression not only contributed deeply to the insecurity with which Americans viewed their economy. It also had an important bearing on economic behaviour. In the years following the Second World War the fear of a recurrence of depression was without question a dominant factor in the calculations of a large proportion of all businessmen. The convention, so scrupulously observed by the business community, which bans the public expression of fear of economic collapse lest to express fear be to invite the fact, concealed much of this alarm. None the less, when *Fortune* magazine in 1946 asked some 15,000 leading business executives in confidence whether they expected an 'extended major depression with large-scale unemployment in the next ten years' – a phrasing that was not designed to minimize the scope of the contemplated disaster – fifty-eight per cent of those replying said they did. Of the remainder only twenty-eight per cent said they did not.* In these same years labour was preoccupied with measures to maintain the level of employment and farmers with support prices that would provide shelter in a slump. Even the radicals had long ceased to talk about the inequality or exploitation under capitalism or its 'inherent contradictions'. They stressed only the utter unreliability of its performance.

These attitudes have since changed. With prosperity and the passage of time the fear of depression has been somewhat dulled. In 1949 and again in 1954 there were minor setbacks, which were first viewed as the beginning of a new disaster but from which there was a prompt recovery. These provided more reassurance. The convention which requires businessmen and politicians who are in office to say that all will always be well – that at any time prosperity is assured – has brought a rich yield of optimism. This too has had an effect.

It has been the custom of economists to take people, and their attitudes, aspirations, hopes, and fears, as given and much the same from one generation to the next. It seems certain that changes in these attitudes are of deep importance. The

* *Fortune*, February 1947, p. 34. The rest declined to say.

rest of this chapter deals with the attitudes that were shaped by the depression. Later, in the final chapter, I venture some observations on the consequences of an escape from the depression psychosis. Fear is no doubt an evil thing. Rarely do we praise it. But I shall argue that the fear of depression favoured us more than we have ever quite supposed.

II

By the mid-thirties, the layman – whether worker, business-man, farmer, or unemployed – had undoubtedly reached his own conclusions concerning American capitalism. Asked were its norm an equilibrium of stable prices and full employ-ment, the conclusion of the competitive model, he would have recommended his interrogator to the care of a good doctor. But, as ideas to be influential need the support of ex-perience, so experience needs interpretation by ideas. Only then does it become the basis for generalization, for a theory. The Great Depression might, conceivably, have remained the great accident if ideas had not again intervened. These, in their mature form, made depression, or its counterpart in-flation, the normal behaviour pattern of uninhibited and unmanaged capitalism. While this discouraging analysis car-ried with it a remedy – a remedy that was received with pro-found enthusiasm by many economists and much of the public at large – the remedy was unorthodox and disturbing. It is only partial comfort for a patient, who is being told he is chronically ill, to learn that there are violent and painful cures for his disease.

The ideas which interpreted the depression, and which warned that depression or inflation might be as much a part of the free-enterprise destiny as stable full employment, were those of John Maynard Keynes. A case could easily be made by those who make such cases that his were the most influential social ideas of the first half of the century. A proper distribution of emphasis as between the role of ideas and the role of action might attribute more influence on modern economic history to Keynes than to Roosevelt. Certainly his final book, *The General Theory of Employment, Interest, and Money*,\* shaped the course of events as only the books of three earlier economists – Smith's *Wealth of Nations*, Ricardo's *Principles of Political Economy* and Marx's *Capital* – have done.

This is a judgement which has the impressive support of Keynes himself. Writing to George Bernard Shaw in early 1935, he said '... I believe myself to be writing a book on economic theory which will largely revolutionize – not, I suppose, at once but in the course of the next ten years – the way the world thinks about economic problems.'† It is not a judgement which greater historical perspective has yet altered.

Keynes's *General Theory* could not normally be read, even by the intelligent layman, unless he was schooled in the language and, even more, in the abstractions of economics. As a result its influence on practical affairs was almost entirely by proxy. It was not from Keynes but from his interpreters at first, second, or third remove that most men learned of his ideas. The interpreters were almost exclusively other economists. Keynes was also beyond the reach of those who do brokerage in fashionable thoughts and, in fact, his ideas gained their ascendancy without creating appreciable stir among intellectuals at large. In any case, millions came to

\* New York: Harcourt, Brace and Co., 1936. Many of the recommendations for public action which emerge from this volume had previously been made by Keynes. However, the general acceptance of Keynes's programme awaited the full development of the underlying *rationale*.

† R. F. Harrod, *The Life of John Maynard Keynes* (New York: Harcourt, Brace and Co., 1951), p. 462.

accept Keynes's conclusions who had never read a word he had written. More interesting, thousands came to be advocates of his proposals who, if asked, would have indignantly denied they were Keynesians. While everyone knows that Keynes was important and influential, there has always been a remarkable uncertainty as to just how or why.

The major conclusion of Keynes's argument – the one of greatest general importance and the one that is relevant here – is that depression and unemployment are in no sense abnormal. (Neither, although the point is made less explicitly, is inflation.) On the contrary, the economy can find its equilibrium at any level of performance. The chance that production in the United States will be at that level where all, or nearly all, willing workers can find jobs is no greater than the chance that four, six, eight, or ten million workers will be unemployed. Alternatively the demand for goods may exceed what the economy can supply even when everyone is employed. Accordingly there can be, even under peacetime conditions, a persistent upward pressure on prices, i.e., more or less serious inflation.

This is not the place to restate Keynes's argument. However, some essentials are necessary for the more constructive tasks of this book which begin with the next chapter. Keynes destroyed, and pretty much without trace, the conclusions that had been derived from Say's Law. The contention that production provided the purchasing power to buy whatever was produced meant that any given level of output was approximately stable. There could be no sudden reduction of output in response to a disappearance of purchasing power.

Output was not completely stable, for, if there happened to be unemployment at the moment, those without work could always make it worth the while of some employer somewhere to hire them by offering to work for less than the going wage. Given the competition of the competitive model, such reductions in wages could occur; the resulting reductions in costs and prices would, it was assumed, lead to an expansion of sales and an increase in employment to a point where all willing workers had jobs.* Thus the equilibrium of the economy tended to be stable only at full employment.

The act of producing and selling a product does, undeniably, place a revenue equivalent to the total value of the article produced in *someone's hands*. The twenty-five hundred dollars that is spent on an automobile does re-emerge as revenue to someone whether in the form of wages, corporate or dealer profits, dividends, salesmen's commissions, repaid debt or revenues to a steel mill to be divided there in turn. It is open to the receiver of this revenue either to spend it or not to spend it. That part which he spends obviously presents

---

* A slightly more technical comment seems called for here. A wage reduction can be of two sorts. It can be confined to those workers who were previously unemployed and who get work by lowering their wage demands. Wages of those already employed remain unaffected. This, of course, is to suppose that the labour market is less than perfect but given this supposition, the effect of these marginal wage reductions in increasing employment is clear. There is no reduction in the general spending in the economy such as would accompany general wage reductions. It is worth the while of employers to add the new, lower-paid workers, and their income provides the wherewithal to buy what they add to production. Something very like this happened in the farm-labour market during the depression and helps explain the continuing full employment in that industry in those years. If it is assumed that the lower wages of the marginal workers bring down all wages, the employment effect is more roundabout. However, if all of the assumptions of the competitive model are rigidly respected, the result is not greatly less certain. Prices will be promptly adjusted to the lower costs; not all of the income flow will be affected by the wage reduction. There will be some substitution of labour for capital. Interest rates will fall, reducing saving. The aggregate effect will be that a somewhat smaller income than before will purchase a larger volume of goods produced (per unit) with more labour. The effect will be higher employment.

no problem. It is spent. It goes back into the market to buy what is produced and so far Say is vindicated.

A failure in ultimate spending must, by definition, arise in that part of the revenue from production which is saved. In the competitive model this was taken care of by the interest rate. On the interest rate was shouldered the heavy task of equating what men were willing to save with what others foresaw they could earn from borrowing and investing such savings. Were savings large and the prospects for returns from new capital investment none too favourable, the rate of interest would fall. This would discourage savers and encourage investors. The smaller volume of savings would be spent for more houses, hydro-electric plants, machine tools, and other investment goods. There would be no loss of purchasing power as the result of the saving.

For many years prior to the appearance of Keynes's *General Theory*, this view of the rate of interest and of its equilibrating function had something of the standing among economists of a folk tale. It had been effectively attacked especially by continental economists. Though it was told to the young and handed on from one generation to the next it would have been hard to find any reputable economist who would admit to believing it completely. There was a general reluctance, even, to expound it in print – Keynes once complained that he could find no full statement of the doctrine which he was attacking.* Yet the conclusion that savings were either invested or otherwise offset which followed from the theory was largely unchallenged. Keynes provided a theory of interest which did not depend on the supply and demand for savings. It was based, instead, on the public's desire to hold money – what he termed its liquidity preference – as against its desire for other and less liquid interest-bearing assets. It is not, in all respects, a plausible alternative

* R. F. Harrod, op. cit., p. 453.

but this was not important. In arguing for his alternative he succeeded, where others had failed, in persuading men of the final inadequacy of the older view of interest, saving, and investment.

The attack on that doctrine – on the marriage of the supply of savings to the amount of investment by way of the interest rate – was what destroyed the old faith in a full-employment equilibrium. If an increase in saving, or more precisely in efforts to save, brings no fall in the interest rate there is no reason to expect that a responding expansion of investment will mop up the extra saving. An increase in investment could only be in response to a decrease in the interest rate; with the connexion between savings and the interest rate broken, interest rates need no longer change with changes in the volume of saving. As a result, an increase in savings could result in a shortage of purchasing power for buying the volume of goods currently being produced. In that case the volume of goods would not continue to be produced. Production and prices would fall; unemployment would increase. This would reduce both savings and spending for current consumption with the probability that, eventually, it would reduce savings the most. At some point such a reduction in total output, with its more than proportionate reduction in savings, would bring savings efforts into balance with investment intentions – despite the fact that investment would probably also have declined meanwhile.* This balance could be at a low level of output and income. Unemployment could be high. And this equilibrium with extensive unemployment might be quite stable.

* Thus between 1929 and 1932 the annual volume of investment in the United States (total gross private domestic investments) fell from $15.8 billion to $900 million. However, savings of individuals (not corporations) declined from $3.7 billion to – $1.4 billion. (Estimates from *The Economic Report of the President*, Council of Economic Advisers, January 1950).

In principle the unemployed man could still find someone to hire him by reducing his wage – and as a practical matter hundreds of thousands of urban workers retreated to agriculture during the depression where they found employment or self-employment by this formula. But there is good reason to question the practicability of such a remedy in an economy which has so far departed from the rigours of the competitive model as to have unions and common wage scales for similar work and workers. Where these exist the individual worker cannot agree, as an individual, to work for less than the going or union rate. There can, of course, be a general wage cut. In the competitive model the lower costs that would result from such a reduction would bring a prompt response in the form of efforts to increase production. This would as promptly bring down prices. Such an adjustment cannot be assumed in markets characterized by oligopoly – markets where prices are administered by a few large sellers.* Thus, in the modern economy, it is at least possible that the loss of purchasing power, resulting from the lower wages for the group, will be greater than the increase in total income resulting from the greater production at the lower costs. With the old explanation as to why depressions could not occur went the faith in the old remedies for the depressions that did none the less occur.

For purpose of displaying the essentials of the Keynesian argument it is convenient to assume an increase in saving and to see what happens – or rather what does not happen. The important consequence is that investment does not necessarily increase in order to absorb the saving; instead total production and employment may be reduced sufficiently to bring reduced saving into line with investment. In practice,

* This is not, strictly speaking, an argument used by Keynes. He had, in fact, a tendency to assume whatever competitive structure best served the purposes of his argument at any given point.

economists have almost uniformly stressed fluctuations in investment rather than changes in saving as the important factor affecting total production. What people will endeavour to save from any given volume of income is commonly supposed to be less subject to change than what business concerns may seek to invest. It has become customary, therefore, to think of changes in investment as the principal cause of changes in total production and employment. Insufficient investment has become the shorthand Keynesian explanation of low production and high unemployment. The obvious remedy is more investment and, in principle, it is not important whether this be from private or public funds. But the expenditure of public funds is subject to central determination by government, as that of private funds is not, so the Keynesian remedy leads directly to public expenditure as a depression remedy.

It is apparent that public spending is only one of the remedies implicit in the Keynesian system. Abatement of taxes in order to leave private individuals more money to spend and measures to stimulate private investment or discourage saving would have a similar effect. However, it is always for his prodigality that a man is known – Henry VIII for his wives, Louis XV for his mistresses, and General Douglas MacArthur for his prose. The Keynesian has become forever associated with public spending.

In principle the Keynesian system is symmetrical. Set against deflation and unemployment is the equal and opposite danger of inflation. Those who make investment decisions may seek to invest more than the community saves even from the incomes which are enjoyed at full employment. A higher interest rate by Keynes's argument does not act to encourage saving – to cause people to cut down on their current consumption and thus make room for investment. If those who control investment decisions are trying to acquire more labour, materials, and other resources than are being spared by savings from current consumption – and if production can no longer be readily expanded because the labour force is fully employed – it is obvious that something must happen. What happens is that prices will go up and people who had no intention of cutting down on consumption – foregoing an automobile in order that steel could be used for a pipeline – find themselves forced to do so because of the advance in prices.

In practice, the Keynesian system was never really accepted as symmetrical. The depression psychosis afflicted economists no less than others. Although the point has been loosely and erroneously made that Keynes was 'a depression economist' it is true that it was in relation to depression that his ideas were most eagerly explored. I shall have occasion to argue later that had there been equally serious discussion of their bearing on inflation, in a world where large corporations exercise measurable control over their prices and bargain with large unions, the Keynesian remedies would not have been found entirely reassuring.

### III

Keynes's impact on the economics of the English-speaking world was prompt and profound. An extension of his central point – that changes in total production and employment are an inherent part of the process by which the economy adjusts itself to movements in investment and savings and that, accordingly, neither depression nor inflation is abnormal – is now widely agreed. Some of the more detailed parts of his argument have been accepted even by those who, initially, most vigorously resisted his ideas. Indeed the protagonist whom Keynes used, somewhat unfairly, as the symbol of all he was attacking in the old system of economics, Professor Pigou of Cambridge University, came eventually to accept much of Keynes and to acknowledge most handsomely his debt.* Keynes's system also provided a firm theoretical basis for the statistical measurement of over-all economic behaviour – for the national accounting which measures the level, content, and changes in total national product – which is now universally employed.†

At the outbreak of the Second World War the new system of national accounting, now generally familiar through its summary figure of Gross National Product, had just come into use in the United States, the United Kingdom, and Canada. It proved indispensable for the guidance of mobilization policy. It had not yet fully penetrated Germany. Partly because they were less clear than the democracies about what they were producing, how they were dividing it between military and civilian use, how they were allocating resources between immediate use and investment, and how the corresponding income was being divided – all information that was displayed by the new accounts – the Germans mobilized their economic resources with considerably less skill and boldness than did England or the United States. Because they are modest men, economists never advertised the power of the weapon they had placed in the hands of their governments although its bearing on victory in that conflict was considerably greater than atomic energy. Perhaps they were wise. Had their wartime significance been fully appreciated, some aggressive patriot would almost certainly have demanded that national income, gross national product, their components and the manner of their calculation, all be made subject to strict security.

* A. C. Pigou, *Keynes' General Theory: A Retrospect* (London: Macmillan Co., 1950).

† Its principal American inventor was Professor Simon Kuznets of the University of Pennsylvania, for whose magnificently conceived statistical measurement Keynes, in effect, provided the underlying theory.

### IV

The time has now come to consider the political consequences of Keynes for, more than any man of the century, he reformulated attitudes on the agitated question of the relation of the state to the economy.

The United States, in the thirties, was urgently in need of a new theory of the relation of government to economic life. The American political parties had long been in the habit of assuming full responsibility for economic well-being and of campaigning with promises of prosperity for all. The inconsistency of these promises, which Republicans and Democrats had made with equal fervour, with the role assigned to the state by the competitive model was untroublesome so long as there was reasonable prosperity in any event. It was bound to be troublesome to a party which was forced to contend with a serious depression. The New Deal came to power on the usual promises and with little clearer view than predecessor administrations of how the government might intervene to bring prosperity.

It was inevitable that the attention of liberals in a liberal administration would be directed towards the structure of the economy. The preconceptions of the competitive model guided their thinking in this direction. Implicit in the rise of big business was the possibility that it had created a structure that departed so far from the competitive model that it could not work. Two courses of action were open. The incentives which, under the competitive model, were presumed to guide businessmen to a socially desirable behaviour could be replaced by some kind of central guidance which would get the desired results. Perhaps businessmen could be brought together under the aegis of government and be told, or made to agree, to increase employment and stabilize wages and prices. Or, alternatively, perhaps private incentives could be rehabilitated by remaking business enterprise so that it conformed more closely to the preconceptions of the model.

Both enterprises involved the most serious difficulties. The first, which was given a trial run in the NRA, suffered from a grievous unclarity of both methods and goals. The self-interest of the businessman dictated the particular low level of employment he was offering and investment he was making in 1933. This simple fact was not altered by bringing him together with other businessmen under the supervision of a Code Authority. It seems improbable that much would have been accomplished had he been ordered directly by government to increase employment and investment outlays at his own cost and contrary to his own assessment of interest.

To remake the economy in accordance with the requirements of the competitive model was obviously a time-consuming enterprise. To take time out to break up large corporate units and re-establish the competition of the model was hardly in keeping with the temper of a country which found depression tiresome and which was not noted for its patience. To the extent that it was contemplated in the later years of the New Deal it was as a decidedly long-run reform. There remained in 1933 only the possibility of abandoning capitalism entirely. This was a project which raised the question of alternatives concerning which only a handful of Communists were in any way clear. It is hardly surprising that the early days of the New Deal were distinguished in American history for their foggy semanticism – for meaningless or incomprehensible talk about social planning, guided capitalism, and industrial self-government. When stumped by a problem the American liberal rarely admits defeat. He takes the offensive with words.

It was Keynes who provided the escape from the dilemma – and the words. It would be hard, at first glance, to imagine a formula that was better designed for the American scene. The depression was overwhelmingly the important problem. The notion of an excess of savings or a deficiency of investment* defined the nature of the government intervention. By public borrowing or expenditure, or the appropriate changes in taxation, the government could make up for the deficiency in private spending. By so doing it could return the economy to full employment and keep it there. To the naked eye, the scope of private business decision remained as before. General Motors still decided what cars to produce, what prices to charge, how to advertise and sell them, when to build a new assembly plant, and how many workers to employ. It merely sold more cars because employees on public works projects became customers for second-hand Chevrolets, their foremen for new ones, and the contractor for a Buick.

The government had always taxed: to reduce taxes and so release income for spending or, perhaps, to adjust taxes to fall more heavily on income that was likely to end up as redundant saving involved no radical departure. The government had always spent. To spend for the express purpose of absorbing savings and raising the level of output and employment in the economy, if novel, was far from revolutionary. The government borrowed for at least part of this expenditure. But the debt so created was the counterpart of private debt that would have been created had private investment absorbed the excess of savings. In any case one strong wing of the Keynesian thought assumed (and the assumption has not yet been entirely abandoned) that periods of unemployment and of inflation would alternate at convenient inter-

---

* More awkwardly, but more accurately, of efforts to save and intentions to invest. By frustrating these efforts and intentions, changes in total output keep savings and investment as Keynes defines them always equal.

vals. Since the formula for periods of inflation seemed to be the simple obverse of that for unemployment – higher taxes, especially on income to be spent, diminished public spending, and a budget surplus – the debts of one period would be liquidated by the excess revenues of the next. The budget would be balanced in accordance with all the canons of fiscal orthodoxy. It was only necessary that a little time elapse.

### V

Liberals almost spontaneously adopted the Keynesian formula. They were also puzzled by the reluctance of conservatives, especially businessmen, to embrace it. Here was protection from the overwhelming threat of depression, the only threat of potentially revolutionary proportions seemingly faced by capitalism. The businessman remained undisturbed in his prerogatives as an owner and manager and had the promise of better business to boot. What could he lose?

With time there has been some explicit and a great deal of implicit acceptance of the Keynesian formula by American businessmen. However, as often happens, it encountered the sharp cleavage which exists in our attitude towards techno-logical and social change. If a man seeks to design a better mousetrap he is the soul of enterprise; if he seeks to design a better society he is a crackpot. For those who mistrust social change it was not an argument that profits might be increased, even that disaster might be avoided. They were opposed to change and they could not be bought. They were men of principle.

There were also more positive grounds for business op-position to Keynes than liberals have been inclined to suppose. The Keynesian system, though it perhaps involved a less than revolutionary change in the relation of the government to the economy, implied, none the less, an important one. For a doctrine that excluded government it substituted one that made government indispensable. Keynes was sufficiently unpalatable when he made depression and inflation not adventitious or war-induced misfortunes but normal occurrences. He went on to make government the indispensable partner of business. In failing to recognize the prestige that goes with power and decision-making in American life, American liberals failed to recognize that, for some businessmen, the Keynesian remedy was at least as damaging as the depression it presumed to eliminate. Even though the businessman might profit in a narrow pecuniary sense from the new role of government there was no chance that his prestige would survive intact. Where, in economic life, people had previously looked upon business decisions as the ones that had shaped their destiny, now they would have regard for government decisions as well, or instead. Those of an Assistant Secretary of the Treasury on interest rates were now of more importance than those of any banker. Those of a regional administrator of public works on investment attained a significance greater than those of a corporation president. To share the prestige of decision-making is to lose prestige. The Keynesian remedies thus represented an assault on a valued possession. Those who were losers could hardly be expected to embrace the ideas that brought this loss. Much of their dissatisfaction was expressed in personal terms – it was directed against the Administration and against the public servants who implemented the new ideas. But a good deal was directed at Keynes. His American followers, taking at face value our conventional disavowal of any interest in power, failed to understand the discontent over its impairment.

The Keynesian system also, though unobtrusively, opened the way for a large expansion of government services and activities. This was the result of a new and very important concept of social waste which followed in its train. If the normal tendency of the economy is towards full employment, then the use of labour and other economic resources by government is at the expense of their use by the private economy. Dams and post offices are built at the cost of private consumption or investment. If there is full employment in the first place, something must be given up. But if unemployment is chronic, the dams and post offices require no sacrifice of private production or consumption. The labour, plants, and materials that are used would otherwise have been unemployed. They are wasted if someone does not employ them. Again ideas had produced a topsy-turvy world. Government spending, long the mark of profligacy, was now sanctioned in the sacred name of avoiding waste. It was inevitable also that wild men would draw from this paradox, and the substantial truths on which it is built, a sanction for any and all expenditures at any and all times. Here was further discomfort for the conservative.

The Keynesian ideas had other new, heterodox, and even threatening corollaries. Thrift, an ancient and once an absolute virtue, was brought into question; it suffered from the guilt of association with redundant saving and depression. A doctrine which cast doubt on so conventional a good was bound to be suspect. We commonly bring a deep theological conviction to the defence of our chosen principles. Those who dissent are not wrong, they are evil. Nothing could better prove that a man was secretly in the service of the devil or communism than that he should raise his voice against thrift.

Finally the new doctrine raised uncomfortable questions concerning both income distribution and profits. Say's Law provided a highly satisfactory defence of incomes and profits even when these were generous. They might not be deserved but, since they were either spent or saved and promptly invested. they did not impair the functioning of the economy.

On the contrary they benefited it. The pressure to consume is least urgent on high personal incomes and high profits; there is the greatest chance of saving from such income and, when invested, this provides the factories, machinery, utilities, and motive power by which future production is increased.

Once saving and the certainty of its utilization in investment became suspect, this defence of high personal incomes and high profits dissolved. More than that, such income became subject to a new attack. If these were the incomes whence the most saving came, it was by these that depressions were caused. By levelling off high incomes and profits one could reduce the amount of savings that had to be offset by investment at full employment. This would promote economic stability.

In the decade following the Second World War business profits were exceedingly handsome – several times what they were before or even during the war. The question of the fairness of these profits and the resulting personal incomes – the question of whether someone was getting more than he deserved – was hardly raised. This was the ancient objection to high profits but it is so no longer. Envy in our time is confined to the contemplation of the privileges or possessions of others of nearly equal income. The post-war attack on profits, as avowed, was almost exclusively on their alleged contribution to instability. It was widely asserted that high profits were the feature of the boom which, if uncurbed, would cause the bust. This also was the handiwork of Keynes.

The disagreements arising out of Keynes's proposals should not be magnified. He was not a divisive figure; on the contrary his work was solidly in the Anglo-American tradition of compromise which seeks progress by reconciling the maximum number of conflicts of interest. But it is also easy to see how his formula, and the speed with which it was accepted, provided its own ground for uneasiness.

## The Depression Psychosis

Enough has now been said of the sources of the insecurity of Americans of varying temper concerning their economy. The time has come to examine the substance of these doubts.

# CHAPTER 7

# The Economics of Technical Development

I

CLEARLY the drift of the accepted and reputable ideas concerning the economy of the United States has been towards a most dismal set of conclusions. They suggest that the economy does not work at its highest efficiency; incentives do not reward most the man who produces what people most want at least cost. The greatest reward may go to the crypto-monopolist or to the most skilful advertiser and salesman. The accepted ideas also expose a disagreeable problem of power. A plenary authority lies with the heads of private corporations, evidently also with leaders of unions, which enables them to make decisions affecting the wealth and livelihood of others. There is no reason for supposing that the economy works reliably. The depression of the thirties remains impressively on the record to suggest the possibility of serious breakdown. The accepted ideas make depression, or its counterpart inflation, as normal as good performance. True, the Keynesian system, which affirms the likelihood of such misfortune, carries with it a remedy. But it is one requiring a degree of government participation in the economy which many conservatives, to put it mildly, find repugnant.

Yet most Americans, and most foreigners whose sources of information bear a perceptible relation to the truth, undoubtedly consider the American economy, as it performed in the years following the Second World War, a considerable success. In principle the economy pleased no one; in practice it satisfied most. Social inefficiency, unrationalized power, intrusive government, and depression were all matters for deep concern. But neither liberals nor conservatives, neither the rich nor all but the very poor, found the consequences intolerable.

Pessimism in our time is infinitely more respectable than optimism: the man who foresees peace, prosperity, and a decline in juvenile delinquency is a negligent and vacuous fellow. The man who foresees trouble – except perhaps on the stock market – has a gift of insight which insures that he will become a radio commentator, an editor of *Time*, or go to Congress. Recognizing the risks in running counter to our national preference for gloom, it may still be worth while to inquire why the years of peace after the Second World War proved tolerable. Conceivably, from this analysis, one can learn how the future can be tolerable too. The task of this and the chapters following is to examine in turn the circumstances which have kept social inefficiency, private power, government intervention, and unemployment from ruining us in the recent present.

II

The first reason the period was tolerable is that efficiency in the American economy appears in a deep disguise. To the man steeped in the preconceptions of the competitive model the disguise is nearly complete. The incentives in the typical American industry, the industry pre-empted by a handful of large firms, do not in fact work in the direction of maximum output at lowest prices. Subject to important restraints, which I will examine later, the market power of the individual firm is used, at any given time, to obtain prices that are higher for an output that, as a result, is smaller than would be ideal. In consumers' goods industries, great energy is, without doubt, channelled into one or another form of selling effort, which is of no perceptible benefit to the public and which is not in response to any recognizable public demand.

However, there is a major compensation for much of this inefficiency, and that is technical change. Moreover, a benign Providence who, so far, has loved us for our worries, has made the modern industry of a few large firms an excellent instrument for inducing technical change. It is admirably equipped for financing technical development. Its organization provides strong incentives for undertaking development and for putting it into use.* The competition of the competitive model, by contrast, almost completely precludes technical development.

There is no more pleasant fiction than that technical change is the product of the matchless ingenuity of the small man forced by competition to employ his wits to better his neighbour. Unhappily, it is a fiction. Technical development has long since become the preserve of the scientist and the engineer. Most of the cheap and simple inventions have, to put it bluntly and unpersuasively, been made. Not only is development now sophisticated and costly but it must be on a sufficient scale so that successes and failures will in some measure average out. Few can afford it if they must expect all projects to pay off. This was not the case in the late eighteenth and the nineteenth century. Then, in the beginning stages of the applications of science and technology to industry and agriculture, there was scope for the uncomplicated ingenuities of a Hargreaves or a Franklin. The competition of the competitive model encouraged such ingenuity

* This point has been much overlooked by economists. A major exception was the late Professor Joseph A. Schumpeter in whose system the innovating role of large enterprises is strongly emphasized. See his *Capitalism, Socialism, and Democracy* (New York: Harper & Bros., 2nd ed., 1943), pp. 79 ff. While my analysis is in a tradition of economic theory different from his, and one of which he was frequently critical, the conclusions on this point are similar.

and assured the spreading of its fruits. As elsewhere the competitive model had great appropriateness to the industrial society which it was meant to interpret. Its designers were not abstruse theorists or dolts. But the society they interpreted has changed.

Because development is costly, it follows that it can be carried on only by a firm that has the resources which are associated with considerable size. Moreover, unless a firm has a substantial share of the market it has no strong incentive to undertake a large expenditure on development. There are, in practice, very few innovations which cannot be imitated – where secrecy or patent protection accords any considerable advantage to the pioneer. Accordingly the competitor of the competitive model must expect that his innovation will be promptly copied or imitated. Whether it be a new product or a new way of reducing the costs of producing an old one, the change will be dispersed over a market in which he has only an infinitely small share. The imitators, who haven't stood the cost of development, profit along with the pioneer. And presently prices will adjust themselves to remove entirely the advantage of the innovator. He is thus restored to a plane of equality with his imitators. Hence the very mechanism which assures the quick spread of any known technology in the purely competitive market, and which was a strong recommendation of that market, eliminates the incentive to technical development itself. It leaves to the pioneer, apart from the rare case of effective patent protection, only the fleeting rewards of a head start. Where the costs of development are considerable, there is no reason to suppose that the returns to the pioneer will be sufficient to compensate for the cost. On the contrary, as the costs of development increase – and with time and progress towards more sophisticated innovation they must increase – there is a diminishing likelihood that they will be recovered. The higher the level of science and technology required for change, the more nearly static an industry which conforms to the competitive model will become.

In the industry that is shared by a relatively small number of large firms, the convention that excludes price competition does not restrain technical innovation. This remains one of the important weapons of market rivalry. The firms, typically, are large. Hence resources are available on a scale appropriate to the modern requirements of technical development. Some of them in fact are the fruits of market power – of monopoly gains. And, while imitation must be assumed and expected, the convention which limits price competition also insures that the returns, whether to a new product or from cost-reducing innovation, will accrue to the innovator as well as to its rivals at least for a period of time. The presence of market power makes the length of this time period subject to some measure of control.

Thus, in the modern industry shared by a few large firms, size and the rewards accruing to market power combine to insure that resources for research and technical development will be available. The power that enables the firm to have some influence on prices insures that the resulting gains will not be passed on to the public by imitators (who have stood none of the costs of development) before the outlay for development can be recouped. In this way market power protects the incentive to technical development.

The net of all this is that there must be some element of monopoly in an industry if it is to be progressive. This, at first glance, is shockingly at variance with accepted notions. Economists have long excoriated the comfortable domination of an industry by a single firm in the belief that such a firm will sit not only on production but on progress as well. So, far from spending money on innovation, it may even suppress patents in order to protect existing investment in plant and machinery.

Such a view of the behaviour of a monopoly may not be entirely in error although, as Schumpeter has argued, it may be somewhat less probable in a world where there are always potential substitutes and where innovation is proceeding elsewhere.* The error has resulted from generalizing from what may be the plausible behaviour of a single firm in possession of the entire output of an industry to the consequences of the monopoly power of a few firms sharing the output of an industry. Because stagnation is a plausible counterpart of monopoly in the first case, it has been thought to be a likely counterpart of the monopoly power that undoubtedly exists in the second case. This generalization, so far from being valid, would appear to be almost completely in error.

To be sure, some room must be left for exceptions. One can imagine that the convention against price competition could be extended, in the industries of small numbers, to innovation. And, as in the well-publicized instances of patent suppression, this has undoubtedly happened. But to maintain a convention against innovation requires a remarkably comprehensive form of collusion. Change involves a great many different things. Agreement must be reached on the kinds to be banned and the kinds to be allowed. Such agreement can hardly, as in the case of prices, be tacit. There must be formal negotiation and this is difficult as well as legally dangerous. While it would be going too far to say that oligopoly insures progress, technical development is all but certain to be one of the instruments of commercial rivalry when the number of firms is small. Like advertising and salesmanship – and unlike price competition which is unique in this respect – technical development is a safe rather than a

* ibid., pp. 101-2.

reciprocally destructive method by which any one firm can advance itself against its few powerful rivals.

Moreover, in a community which sets great store by progress, technical advance is an important source of business prestige. An American business concern simply cannot afford the reputation of being unprogressive. If it has no laboratories it must imagine some; an annual report that makes no reference to research is unthinkable. Such an environment is highly unfavourable to any systematic restraint on innovation.

Thus there can be little doubt that oligopoly, both in theory and in fact, is strongly oriented towards change. There can be no serious doubt at all that the setting for innovation, which is so favourable in this market structure, disappears almost entirely as one approaches the competition of the competitive model.

### III

These propositions can be readily verified by experience. The American farmer, the producer who most closely approaches the competitor of the model, does almost no research on his own behalf. It was the foresight of genius that caused this to be recognized at an early stage in our history, with the result that technical development within this field has been almost completely socialized. We now take for granted that technical development in agriculture as such will come from the State Experiment Stations and from the United States Department of Agriculture. There would be little technical development and not much progress in agriculture were it not for government-supported research supplemented by the research and development work of the corporations which devise and sell products to the farmer. The latter, typically, are in industries characterized by oligopoly. The individual farmer cannot afford a staff of chemists to develop an animal protein factor which makes different proteins interchangeable as feeds. So many would appropriate the innovation so quickly, without having contributed to the cost of development, that it wouldn't profit any farmer to try.

The other industries which are distinguished by a close approach to the competitive model are also distinguished, one can almost say without exception, by a near absence of research and technical development. The bituminous coal industry, apart from a handful of very large operators; the cotton textile industry, apart from a few very large groups of mills; the clothing industry, the lumber industry, and the shoe industry do very little research. None of them is thought of as a technically progressive industry. All of them (apart always from the few large firms they contain and which help prove the case) roughly meet the specifications of the competitive model. They also conform to the ideal which the American economist has had anciently in mind. No firm in these industries (the few special cases again excepted) has appreciable influence on prices; each is forced by circumstances which it cannot control to search for the greatest efficiency of operation; in most of them entry and exit are admirably free; few of the firms in these industries engage in extensive competitive advertising and salesmanship. Yet almost no one would select them as a showpiece of American industrial achievement. The showpieces are, with rare exceptions, the industries which are dominated by a handful of large firms. The foreign visitor, brought to the United States to study American production methods and associated marvels, visits the same firms as do attorneys of the Department of Justice in their search for monopoly.

The reductions in cost, and the consequent increases in efficiency from technical change, can be of a wholly different order of magnitude from those sacrificed as the result of the exercise of market power. Thus it comes about that a slight continuing loss of efficiency, as compared with ideal performance, from the possession of market power is regularly offset and more than offset by large gains from technical development. Economists, aided by the new market theory, have fixed their attention on the loss and have overlooked the offset. In concentrating on the inefficiency of the steam engine – specifically the fact that it is not being worked at ideal capacity – they have failed to notice that the owner was designing a gas turbine.

IV

A comparison of the oil with the bituminous coal industry usefully illustrates the point being emphasized. The oil industry is an unquestioned oligopoly; in any market area there are a few large firms and the characteristic fringe of independents. Over the years it has been under repeated attack for violation of the antitrust laws; it has rarely been free of suspicion of holding prices above the level that would be associated with more vigorous price competition. Profits have generally been excellent. Yet few would be inclined to trade the oil industry for the bituminous coal industry which, abstracting from possible stabilization efforts by the United Mine Workers, approaches the competition of the model.

The oil industry is clearly progressive – almost as progressive, perhaps, as the uncommonly attractive brochures of its member companies unreluctantly concede. As the result of its enterprise in petroleum exploration and recovery, in developing new products, and in engineering new methods of transporting both petroleum and products, the consumer of gasoline and fuel oil has been a far more fortunate man than the consumer of coal. The continuing shift of customers from the admirably competitive coal industry to the dubiously competitive oil industry emphasizes the point.

It seems reasonable to suppose that if the same technical talent that has been devoted to the search for oil, or to its utilization, had been brought to bear on coal-mining in the last half-century, the coal industry would be very different from what it is today. New techniques of recovery might long since have been developed. Men would no longer toil like moles in mining operations that 'under the most favourable conditions are hazardous and highly inefficient ... an unpleasant, uninspiring, and none too healthy occupation'.* It is significant, by way of verifying the technical limitations of competition, that some modern efforts to raise the technology of coal production have required the cooperative effort of the industry and that the significant work on the hydrogenation of coal has been under government sponsorship. In other words the limitations inherent in the individual competitive unit had to be finessed. One of the country's experienced research administrators has observed of the coal industry that 'An industry with 6,000 little units has made a terribly difficult pattern on which to develop modern industrial research programmes.'†

V

Thus, while the incentives in the American economy do not, at any given moment, act to encourage the largest possible production at the lowest possible price, this is not the tragedy that it appears to be at first glance. The market concentra-

* 'Coal I: The Industrial Darkness,' *Fortune*, March 1947. Quoted from *Industrial Engineering and Chemistry*, August 1946.

† Frank A. Howard, ibid., p. 87. It must be observed that the anthracite industry, the ownership of which is considerably more concentrated than bituminous mining, has not, at least until recent times, been credited with any visibly progressive tendencies. There appear, however, to have been special reasons, relating generally to character of ownership, for this.

tion of American industry that is affirmed by the statistics and condemned by the competitive model turns out on closer examination to be favourable to technical change. To get the ideal equilibrium of price and output of the competitive model, we should almost certainly have to forego the change. Life might be simpler were we to do so, but progress, as it is called, is a wheel to which we are all bound.

In all this there is less comfort for the businessman than might appear. He must still defend himself from the charge that he is too big and that he is partially monopolistic with the reply that he is really competitive in the classical sense. In the words of a leading oil company, speaking recently of the Gulf Coast refining market, he must aver that in his industry the 'truest, finest form of competitive pricing exists.'* For competition, with us, is more than a technical concept. It is also a symbol of all that is good. We wouldn't survive under a régime of competition of classical purity – with an economy rigorously so characterized we should have succumbed not to Hitler but to Wilhelm II – but we must still worship at its throne.

* *Competition Makes Gasoline Prices* (Philadelphia: Sun Oil Company, n.d.).

# CHAPTER 8

# The Unseemly Economics of Opulence

I

THERE is a deeply held belief, the Puritan antecedents of which are clear, that if a wealthy man admits even to himself that he can afford a measure of recklessness in his expenditures, an angry God will strike him dead – or certainly take away his money. This holds also for nations. The utmost reticence must be observed in talking about the affluence of the United States. It is permissible to concede, even with a certain amount of pride, that the United States is a wealthy country. But to conclude that in peacetime this opulence excuses a certain amount of social waste is to invite the divine fury that immolated Sodom and Gomorrah. Yet a great many things about the United States can be explained only by its wealth. Although economists have long respected the taboo on drawing conclusions from it, in the service of science certain risks must now be run.

Not even the genius of the adman has been wholly equal to the task of proving that the paper, ether, and skills employed in, say, cigarette advertising are related to any urgent public need. As with cigarette advertising so, presumably, with highway billboards, redundant service stations, glossy packages, bread that is first denatured and then fortified, high-pressure salesmanship, singing commercials, and the concept of the captive audience. All, in one way or another, are apparently the result of incentives which guide the energies of men not towards but away from maximum social efficiency. Few would insist that these activities are in response to any very pressing desire of the American people. This is the criterion of efficiency of the competitive model. By this standard the American economy is undoubtedly a wasteful one.

However, much of the criticism of the vast activity of selling and advertising in the American economy – that which concerns economics rather than taste or the devastation of the countryside by billboards – has missed the point. Economists and a good many others have pointed to the energies devoted to it with shock or alarm. Those who make their living by it have replied, both in anger and in sorrow, that it isn't wasteful at all. Some bold spirits, with a knack for generalization, have said that all critics of selling expenditure are subversive. The truth does not lie in between but elsewhere. Our proliferation of selling activity is the counterpart of comparative opulence. Much of it is inevitable with high levels of well-being. It may be waste but it is waste that exists because the community is too well off to care.

## II

In a country where, as the result of maximum exertion of all, only a bare minimum of food, clothing, fuel, and shelter can be provided, it would indeed be intolerable to have some firms or industries tacitly restricting production and sustaining prices. The price of such a monopoly in, say, the coal-mining industry would be an insufficiency of coal in relation to what consumers desperately need. This might be partially offset by a somewhat greater supply of food. The men and resources who, under more ideal circumstances, would be employed in the mines, would, as the result of the restriction there, find employment in agriculture. But the consequences for the insufficiently heated public would be far from ideal.

Similarly such a community could ill afford to have any considerable fraction of its labour force concocting sales slogans for its limited supply of bread, writing advertising copy for its meagre stock of clothing, putting its few vegetables into cellophane packages, or otherwise bringing the arts of direct salesmanship to bear on its poverty-stricken consumers. In such a land the whole force, male and female, of J. Walter Thompson, Du Pont Cellophane, and the market research firm of Mr Elmo Roper should without question be at work producing potatoes, beans, and coal so that people might be slightly less hungry and cold.

In fact, in such a community, this labour (perhaps after an appropriate rehabilitation for manual employments) would have no choice but to seek these utilitarian occupations. It is not necessary to advertise food to hungry people, fuel to cold people, or houses to the homeless. No one could make a living doing so. The need and the opportunity to persuade people arise only as people have the income to satisfy relatively unimportant wants, of the urgency of which they are not automatically aware. In other words the social inefficiency of a wealthy community grows with the growth in wealth that goes far to make this inefficiency inconsequential.

Thus, while the forty-two million dollars worth of skill, art, and paper spent in 1949 for cigarette advertising and the twenty-nine million dollars devoted to alcoholic beverages served no urgent social purpose the same is true of the cigarettes and the liquor. It is not clear that the community would be better off if those now engaged in selling tobacco and liquor were employed instead in the production of more and cheaper cigarettes and whisky. (Both the alcoholic and the cigarette hangover seem now to be sufficiently institutionalized.) It is not certain, always assuming peace, that Mr James H. Blandings* and the other employees of Banton and

* For those so unfortunate as not to have encountered him, Mr Blandings is an advertising man of incredibly complex personality who lives in the pages of two wise and joyful novels by Eric Hodgins.

Dascomb are needed in any alternative employment – they are not needed, as recent history has shown, in the production of wheat. The alternative use of the resources which a wealthy community appears to use frivolously will always be in other frivolous employments. It will be in the production of things of no very great consequence by any standards.

### III

It will be worth while to examine a little more closely the relation of advertising and selling expenditures to a state of relatively high opulence. These expenditures are made for a variety of purposes. The department stores advertise for no more complex purpose than to let customers know what they have, what they would especially like to sell at the moment, and at what prices. The same motive lies behind an appreciable amount of consumers' goods selling in general. In one way or another the vendor has always had to cry his wares; the modern techniques that are brought to the service of this particular task may be no more costly or no more raucous than those that have been used throughout time.

This kind of salesmanship invites no comment on grounds of social efficiency. Indeed the New York housewife who was forced to do without Macy's advertising would have a sense of loss second only to that from doing without Macy's. However, in a consumers' goods industry shared by a comparatively small number of sellers – the characteristic industry of the contemporary American economy – advertising and selling activity is assumed in modern economics to be undertaken for one or both of two further purposes. It may be, simply, an instrument of commercial rivalry. Price competition having been foresworn as self-destructive, the firm turns to its salesmen and advertising agency to find new customers and to win customers away from its rivals. The firm is seeking, in the economist's terms, to move its demand curve to the right. Such an effort to get more is necessary, in a world where others are doing the same, if the firm is merely to hold its own. Only the very disingenuous can suppose, or argue, that this form of selling effort is just to make the customer aware that the firm has something to sell. Americans would indeed be mentally retarded if they still had to be advised that the American Tobacco Company has Lucky Strikes to dispose of.

It is also generally agreed that the firm may be seeking, often implicitly, through its advertising and salesmanship so to establish its own personality that it will be protected in some measure from other firms which do not reliably observe the convention against price competition. If a firm is able to persuade the public that its brand of toothpaste, pancake flour, razor blades, or aspirin has qualities that are unique, or if it can merely get shoppers to name its brand without thought when they go into a store, then it is somewhat protected from the rivalry of other firms who sell the same product at a lower price. In so enhancing the market power which it has over its own brand, it acquires some freedom to move its own price without inviting loss of custom. The price cuts of other firms can be viewed with some equanimity. Economic theory has given much attention to this process of 'product differentiation' in recent times. As a motive, either overt or implicit, for advertising and other selling expenditure its importance has been considerably exaggerated. Simple rivalry between firms is almost certainly far more important. Still, it is a recognizable phenomenon and the wastes associated with efforts to build up brand monopolies have been greatly deplored.

There could be no great volume of selling expenditure of either of these sorts, except in a wealthy community. In such a community the money dispensed in any given purchase is not of high importance to the person spending it – in the language of economics, the marginal utility of money is low. In such a community, also, a great many different purchases are made by each individual. The result is that no single purchase is worth a great deal of thought; there are too many of them for each to be considered in detail. Accordingly the purchaser is a ready subject for the attentions of the advertiser and the salesman. He even allows himself to be influenced by imaginary or contrived virtues, because he is not sufficiently under the pressure of want to learn whether or not these virtues are imaginary. He yields to the influence of suggestion because he is not obliged, by want, to think about his actions. On going into a store he repeats a brand name that has been iterated and reiterated over the radio or on television because the money he is spending is not of sufficient importance to justify his ascertaining whether there are better and cheaper alternatives. Those who are persuaded that the buyer is victimized need to realize that, in the first instance, he is the victim of his own comparative well-being.

The opportunity for product differentiation – for associating monopoly power with the brand or personality of a particular seller – is almost uniquely the result of opulence. A hungry man could never be persuaded that bread that is softened, sliced, wrapped, and enriched is worth more than a cheaper and larger loaf that will fill his stomach. A southern cropper will not, as the result of advertising, develop a preference for one brand of cooked, spiced, and canned ham over another. He will continue to buy plain sidemeat. No one would advertise the sound-effects of processed breakfast foods striking the milk to Scottish crofters who have only the resources to buy oatmeal. In such communities all the commercial advantages lie with the producers of plain bread, sidemeat and oatmeal.

The tendency for other forms of commercial rivalries, as substitutes for price competition, to be channelled into advertising and salesmanship would disappear in a poor community. One cannot be certain that the convention against price competition itself could be maintained. The nicotine addict, who now automatically buys one or another of the standard brands of cigarettes, would, under the whiplash of necessity, become an inviting market for a cheaper product. The firm that provided it would acquire customers with a rush. Something very like this happened during the early years of the depression when millions of impoverished smokers turned enthusiastically to the ten-cent brands of cigarettes. In any case, for maintaining the convention against price competition, it is a great help to have customers who do not care – even if, on occasion, they think they do.

There is a legend, with a great appeal to simple men, that Americans are a nation of salesmen because they have some peculiar virtuosity in this craft. There are more salesmen, and salesmanship is more highly developed, in the United States than elsewhere in the world. But the explanation lies not with national character but with national wealth. The latter means, of course, that there are more goods to be sold. But even more, it means that psychological, not physical, considerations control desire. The biological minimums are covered. As a result that modern practitioner of applied psychology, the salesman, gets his opportunity. Sent to practise on Indians or Chinese or even French peasants the most brilliant American vendor would be a dismal failure.

Many of my fellow economists will have difficulty in sharing the equanimity with which I here view selling costs and the so-called wastes of distribution. Economics began in the eighteenth and nineteenth centuries when men were really poor. Two of its great pioneers, Malthus and Ricardo, held that grinding poverty was the fate of man – any surplus wealth, above the requirements for bare subsistence, would be promptly absorbed into the additional mouths that wealth itself would spawn. In such a society inefficiency was, indeed, an evil thing.

It denied bread to the hungry and clothing to the naked even though, if these became available, they launched a new cycle of conception and birth that re-established the common poverty. Western man, as the result of an unsuspected preference for comfort over procreation, and aided by some inexpensive appliances, has escaped from this cycle of poverty. In the United States, in recent times, for most people the biological minimums of food, clothing, and even shelter have been covered as a matter of course. By comparison, the further wants are comparatively unimportant. Economists, none the less, have stuck firmly to their conviction that anything that denies the community additional goods or services, however casual their significance, is the greatest of sins. They have brought the mentality of nineteenth-century poverty to the analysis of twentieth-century opulence.

The result is an inefficient deployment of the economist's own resources. He is excessively preoccupied with goods *qua* goods; in his preoccupation with goods he has not paused to reflect on the relative unimportance of the goods with which he is preoccupied. He worries far too much about partially monopolized prices or excessive advertising and selling costs for tobacco, liquor, chocolates, automobiles, and soap in a land which is already suffering from nicotine poisoning and alcoholism, which is nutritionally gorged with sugar, which is filling its hospitals and cemeteries with those who have been maimed or murdered on its highways, and which is dangerously neurotic about normal body odours.

IV

It is now time to relent slightly and make some needed overtures to orthodoxy. The purpose of the last and the present chapter has been to ascertain how, in spite of the apparent inefficiencies of the American economy, we still manage to survive. We survive partly because we have failed fully to appreciate the extraordinarily high efficiency of technical change and the extraordinarily favourable organization of the economy for inducing it and partly because social efficiency itself has been overemphasized in an economy which has escaped far above the poverty line. This is not a mandate for a total neglect of efficiency. For one thing, there are still many poor people in the United States. They bear the higher prices associated with monopoly power and the higher costs of distribution along with those who can afford them and who, as the result of their escape from physical to psychological standards of consumption, actually encourage such expenditure. There are still many who would live fuller and better lives if elementary goods were produced more abundantly and more cheaply. Housing is a case in point.

Furthermore, the counterpart of monopoly power, if uncorrected by forces I shall examine in the next chapter, is an unsatisfactory allocation of labour and other resources between industries and an unnecessary inequality in the distribution of personal incomes.

The effect of monopoly power on the use of resources has classically been supposed to result in too little employment in the monopolized industries. There is some evidence that in the United States the most damaging effect is, in fact, in encouraging excessive employment in the competitive industries. This part of the economy provides special opportunities to the man who is seeking employment or to employ himself. In the competitive model he can always get employment by sufficiently lowering his wage; where there are parts of the economy, like agriculture, which still conform to the model, these offer that valued opportunity to the independent job seeker. There is a strong possibility, especially when there is less than full employment in the economy, that these industries will attract a heavy surplus of workers. By crowding into this part of the economy they lower, unduly, the returns to those already there. This has been the fate of American agriculture in the past and perhaps also of the textile, clothing, and needlework trades.

In agriculture the problem has been made especially acute by a higher birth rate than in the cities which requires that there be a steady migration to the cities if any given ratio of rural to urban employment is to be maintained. During the depression years the farm-labour force grew substantially as the result of the virtual stoppage of migration to the cities and the return of those who had previously migrated. Even in more favourable times, overemployment in agriculture raises serious problems of maintaining standards of education, health, and welfare at civilized levels in the regions of dense rural population.

In one way or another nearly all of the great American fortunes are based on the present or past possession of monopoly power. It is to oil, railroads, steel, copper, urban real estate, that yesterday's fortunes and the higher of today's unearned incomes trace. Agriculture, bituminous-coal mining, textile and clothing manufacture, have produced few men of great wealth. Income inequality, like monopoly, distorts the use of resources. It diverts them from the wants of the many to the esoteric desires of the few – if not from bread to cake at least from Chevrolets to Cadillacs. Unnecessary inequality in income – unnecessary in the sense that it does not reward differences in intelligence, application, or willingness to take risks – may also impair economic stability. The saving or spending of income that accrues in large chunks to relatively few people is subject to far more erratic impulses than the saving or spending of income of wage and salary earners. Accordingly, there are good reasons for continuing to worry about social inefficiency. At the same time no one should be at loss as to why we survive it.

V

Before taking leave of the unseemly subject of opulence, one of its further consequences must be observed. There is a widely held view that the economic management of the United States is a task requiring the utmost wisdom and subtlety. As a corollary, the utmost peril is implicit in every government decision. Brave men shudder at the consequences of reducing taxes and also of not reducing them; at the increasing burdens of government and also at the failure of the government to assume its proper responsibilities; at the danger of reducing tariffs and the danger of not doing so; at the heavy costs of storing surplus farm products and the danger of not sufficiently protecting the farmer from adversity.

The time may come when the strength of the American economy will turn on the quality of such government decisions but it will be in war or under the threat of war. It has not turned on them in the past. The consequences for general economic welfare of most government decisions has been imperceptible. The first reason is our nearly universal tendency to confuse close decisions with important ones. The most difficult decisions are, normally, the least important. They involve a choice between courses of action which are almost equally favourable – or, on occasion, almost equally unhappy. Different men assess the effects of the alternative courses of action differently and the very closeness of the outcome causes them to marshal their arguments elaborately. Our much-used dialectic of exaggeration is also brought liberally to bear in the argument. Infinite benefit is pictured for one course, utter disaster for another. Were the choice in fact between great good and great damage, it would be so obvious that it would not normally be debated.

The other reason that government decisions have been

relatively unimportant is that we have frequently been able to choose the wrong course rather than the right one because wealth has acted as a solvent for such error. None of the real sources of well-being – the endowment of physical resources and the education and energy of the people – is ever seriously compromised by any government decision. Hence, while unwise government decisions may, in the past, have affected the rate of economic growth, it has been but rarely that one could identify their consequences. This is at least implicitly recognized. Alarm over pending actions by government on economic matters, which frequently reaches almost pathological proportions when the decision is pending, almost invariably evaporates completely once the action is taken.

Wisdom in economic policy is not to be deplored. But one of the profound sources of American strength has been the margin for error provided by our well-being. In the United Kingdom, especially in modern times, there has been little latitude for mistakes. Government management of economic affairs has had, accordingly, to be far more precise than it has ever been with us. An average Congress occupying the House of Commons and functioning in accustomed fashion would, on numerous recent occasions, have brought about a fairly prompt liquidation of what remains of the British Empire.

Wealth does more than provide a margin for error. In the United Kingdom and other Western European countries, social reform – the provision of additional income, services, and security for the underprivileged – has been at the fairly direct expense of the privileged. The clash of interest between those who have and those who have not is obvious and inescapable. With the single exception of the emancipation of the slaves, no measure for the assistance of any group in the United States has brought an *identifiable* reduction in the income of any other group. The costs of free education, social security, assistance to farmers, and like measures of domestic welfare have been deeply disguised by the general increase in income. (In modern times they have also been small in comparison with the far greater costs of defence and war.) Had the assessment of these costs been directly against the static incomes of those who paid but did not benefit, the debate concerning them would have been a good deal more bitter than it was. Wealth, and especially growing wealth, has not only been a solvent for mistakes. It has also been a solvent for what, in its absence, might have been grave social strains.

CHAPTER 9

# The Theory of Countervailing Power

I

ON the night of 2 November 1907, the elder Morgan played solitaire in his library while the panic gripped Wall Street. Then, when the other bankers had divided up the cost of saving the tottering Trust Company of America, he presided at the signing of the agreement, authorized the purchase of the Tennessee Coal & Iron Company by the Steel Corporation to encourage the market, cleared the transaction with President Roosevelt, and the panic was over. There, as legend has preserved and doubtless improved the story, was a man with power a self-respecting man could fear.

A mere two decades later, in the crash of 1929, it was evident that the Wall Street bankers were as helpless as everyone else. Their effort in the autumn of that year to check the collapse in the market is now recalled as an amusing anecdote; the heads of the New York Stock Exchange and the National City Bank fell into the toils of the law and the first went to prison; the son of the Great Morgan went to a Congressional hearing in Washington and acquired fame, not for his authority, but for his embarrassment when a circus midget was placed on his knee.

As the banker, as a symbol of economic power, passed into the shadows his place was taken by the giant industrial corporation. The substitute was much more plausible. The association of power with the banker had always depended on the somewhat tenuous belief in a 'money trust' – on the notion that the means for financing the initiation and expansion of business enterprises was concentrated in the hands of a few men. The ancestry of this idea was in Marx's doctrine of finance capital; it was not susceptible to statistical or other empirical verification at least in the United States.

By contrast, the fact that a substantial proportion of all production was concentrated in the hands of a relatively small number of huge firms was readily verified. That three or four giant firms in an industry might exercise power analogous to that of a monopoly, and not different in consequences, was an idea that had come to have the most respectable of ancestry in classical economics. So as the J. P. Morgan Company left the stage, it was replaced by the two hundred largest corporations – giant devils in company strength. Here was economic power identified by the greatest and most conservative tradition in economic theory. Here was power to control the prices the citizen paid, the wages he received, and which interposed the most formidable of obstacles of size and experience to the aspiring new firm. What more might it accomplish were it to turn its vast resources to corrupting politics and controlling access to public opinion?

Yet, as was so dramatically revealed to be the case with the omnipotence of the banker in 1929, there are considerable gaps between the myth and the fact. The comparative importance of a small number of great corporations in the American economy cannot be denied except by those who have a singular immunity to statistical evidence or striking capacity to manipulate it. In principle the American is controlled, livelihood and soul, by the large corporation; in practice he seems not to be completely enslaved. Once again the danger is in the future; the present seems still tolerable. Once again there may be lessons from the present which, if learned, will save us in the future.

II

As with social efficiency, and its neglect of technical dynamics, the paradox of the unexercised power of the large corporation begins with an important oversight in the underlying economic theory. In the competitive model – the economy of many sellers each with a small share of the total market – the restraint on the private exercise of economic power was provided by other firms on the same side of the market. It was the eagerness of competitors to sell, not the complaints of buyers, that saved the latter from spoliation. It was assumed, no doubt accurately, that the nineteenth-century textile manufacturer who overcharged for his product would promptly lose his market to another manufacturer who did not. If all manufacturers found themselves in a position where they could exploit a strong demand, and mark up their prices accordingly, there would soon be an inflow of new competitors. The resulting increase in supply would bring prices and profits back to normal.

As with the seller who was tempted to use his economic power against the customer, so with the buyer who was tempted to use it against his labour or suppliers. The man who paid less than the prevailing wage would lose his labour force to those who paid the worker his full (marginal) contribution to the earnings of the firm. In all cases the incentive to socially desirable behaviour was provided by the competitor. It was to the same side of the market – the restraint of sellers by other sellers and of buyers by other buyers, in other words to competition – that economists came to look for the self-regulatory mechanism of the economy.

They also came to look to competition exclusively and in formal theory still do. The notion that there might be another regulatory mechanism in the economy has been almost completely excluded from economic thought. Thus, with the widespread disappearance of competition in its classical form and its replacement by the small group of firms if not in overt, at least in conventional or tacit collusion, it was easy to suppose that since competition had disappeared, all effective restraint on private power had disappeared. Indeed this conclusion was all but inevitable if no search was made for other restraints and so complete was the preoccupation with competition that none was made.

In fact, new restraints on private power did appear to replace competition. They were nurtured by the same process of concentration which impaired or destroyed competition. But they appeared not on the same side of the market but on the opposite side, not with competitors but with customers or suppliers. It will be convenient to have a name for this counterpart of competition and I shall call it *countervailing power*.*

To begin with a broad and somewhat too dogmatically stated proposition, private economic power is held in check by the countervailing power of those who are subject to it. The first begets the second. The long trend towards concentration of industrial enterprise in the hands of a relatively few firms has brought into existence not only strong sellers, as economists have supposed, but also strong buyers as they have failed to see. The two develop together, not in precise step but in such manner that there can be no doubt that the one is in response to the other.

The fact that a seller enjoys a measure of monopoly power, and is reaping a measure of monopoly return as a result, means that there is an inducement to those firms from whom he buys or those to whom he sells to develop the power with which they can defend themselves against exploitation. It means also that there is a reward to them, in the form of a share of the gains of their opponents' market power, if they are able to do so. In this way the existence of market power creates an incentive to

* I have been tempted to coin a new word for this which would have the same convenience as the term competition and had I done so my choice would have been 'countervailence'. However, the phrase 'countervailing power' is more descriptive and does not have the raw sound of any newly fabricated word.

the organization of another position of power that neutralizes it.

The contention I am here making is a formidable one. It comes to this: Competition which, at least since the time of Adam Smith, has been viewed as the autonomous regulator of economic activity and as the only available regulatory mechanism apart from the state, has, in fact, been superseded. Not entirely, to be sure. I should like to be explicit on this point. Competition still plays a role. There are still important markets where the power of the firm as (say) a seller is checked or circumscribed by those who provide a similar or a substitute product or service. This, in the broadest sense that can be meaningful, is the meaning of competition. The role of the buyer on the other side of such markets is essentially a passive one. It consists in looking for, perhaps asking for, and responding to the best bargain. The active restraint is provided by the competitor who offers, or threatens to offer, a better bargain. However, this is not the only or even the typical restraint on the exercise of economic power. In the typical modern market of few sellers, the active restraint is provided not by competitors but from the other side of the market by strong buyers. Given the convention against price competition, it is the role of the competitor that becomes passive in these markets.

It was always one of the basic presuppositions of competition that market power exercised in its absence would invite the competitors who would eliminate such exercise of power. The profits of a monopoly position inspired competitors to try for a share. In other words competition was regarded as a *self-generating* regulatory force. The doubt whether this was in fact so after a market had been pre-empted by a few large sellers, after entry of new firms had become difficult and after existing firms had accepted a convention against price competition, was what destroyed the faith in competition as a regulatory mechanism. Countervailing power is also a self-generating force and this is a matter of great importance. Something, although not very much, could be claimed for the regulatory role of the strong buyer in relation to the market power of sellers, did it happen that, as an accident of economic development, such strong buyers were frequently juxtaposed to strong sellers. However the tendency of power to be organized in response to a given position of power is the vital characteristic of the phenomenon I am here identifying. As noted, power on one side of a market creates both the need for, and the prospect of reward to, the exercise of countervailing power from the other side.* This means that, as a common rule, we can rely on countervailing power to appear as a curb on economic power. There are also, it should be added, circumstances in which it does not appear or is effectively prevented from appearing. To these I shall return. For some reason, critics of the theory have seized with particular avidity on these exceptions to deny the existence of the phenomenon itself. It is plain that by a similar line of argument one could deny the existence of competition by finding one monopoly.

In the market of small numbers or oligopoly, the practical barriers to entry and the convention against price competition have eliminated the self-generating capacity of competition. The self-generating tendency of countervailing power, by

* This has been one of the reasons I have rejected the terminology of bilateral monopoly in characterizing this phenomenon. As bilateral monopoly is treated in economic literature, it is an adventitious occurrence. This, obviously, misses the point and it is one of the reasons that the investigations of bilateral monopoly, which one would have thought might have been an avenue to the regulatory mechanisms here isolated, have in fact been a blind alley. However, this line of investigation has also been sterilized by the confining formality of the assumptions of monopolistic and (more rarely) oligopolistic motivation and behaviour with which it has been approached. (Cf. for example, William H. Nicholls, *Imperfect Competition within Agricultural Industries*, Ames, Iowa: 1941, pp. 58ff.) As noted later, oligopoly facilitates the exercise of countervailing market power by enabling the strong buyer to play one seller off against another.

contrast, is readily assimilated to the common sense of the situation and its existence, once we have learned to look for it, is readily subject to empirical observation.

Market power can be exercised by strong buyers against weak sellers as well as by strong sellers against weak buyers. In the competitive model, competition acted as a restraint on both kinds of exercise of power. This is also the case with countervailing power. In turning to its practical manifestations, it will be convenient, in fact, to begin with a case where it is exercised by weak sellers against strong buyers.

### III

The operation of countervailing power is to be seen with the greatest clarity in the labour market where it is also most fully developed. Because of his comparative immobility, the individual worker has long been highly vulnerable to private economic power. The customer of any particular steel mill, at the turn of the century, could always take himself elsewhere if he felt he was being overcharged. Or he could exercise his sovereign privilege of not buying steel at all. The worker had no comparable freedom if he felt he was being underpaid. Normally he could not move and he had to have work. Not often has the power of one man over another been used more callously than in the American labour market after the rise of the large corporation. As late as the early twenties, the steel industry worked a twelve-hour day and seventy-two-hour week with an incredible twenty-four-hour stint every fortnight when the shift changed.

No such power is exercised today and for the reason that its earlier exercise stimulated the counteraction that brought it to an end. In the ultimate sense it was the power of the steel industry, not the organizing abilities of John L. Lewis and

## The Theory of Countervailing Power

Philip Murray, that brought the United Steel Workers into being. The economic power that the worker faced in the sale of his labour – the competition of many sellers dealing with few buyers – made it necessary that he organize for his own protection. There were rewards to the power of the steel companies in which, when he had successfully developed countervailing power, he could share.

As a general though not invariable rule one finds the strongest unions in the United States where markets are served by strong corporations. And it is not an accident that the large automobile, steel, electrical, rubber, farm-machinery, and non-ferrous metal-mining and smelting companies all bargain with powerful unions. Not only has the strength of the corporations in these industries made it necessary for workers to develop the protection of countervailing power; it has provided unions with the opportunity for getting something more as well. If successful they could share in the fruits of the corporation's market power. By contrast there is not a single union of any consequence in American agriculture, the country's closest approach to the competitive model. The reason lies not in the difficulties in organization; these are considerable, but greater difficulties in organization have been overcome. The reason is that the farmer has not possessed any power over his labour force, and at least until recent times has not had any rewards from market power which it was worth the while of a union to seek. As an interesting verification of the point, in the Great Valley of California, the large farmers of that area have had considerable power *vis-à-vis* their labour force. Almost uniquely in the United States, that region has been marked by persistent attempts at organization by farm workers.

Elsewhere in industries which approach the competition of the model, one typically finds weaker or less comprehensive unions. The textile industry,* boot and shoe manufacture, lumbering and other forest industries in most parts of the country, and smaller wholesale and retail enterprises, are all cases in point. I do not, of course, advance the theory of countervailing power as a monolithic explanation of trade-union organization. No such complex social phenomenon is likely to have any single, simple explanation. American trade unions developed in the face of the implacable hostility, not alone of employers, but often of the community as well. In this environment organization of the skilled crafts was much easier than the average, which undoubtedly explains the earlier appearance of durable unions here. In the modern bituminous coal-mining and more clearly in the clothing industry, unions have another explanation. They have emerged as a supplement to the weak market position of the operators and manufacturers. They have assumed price- and market-regulating functions that are the normal functions of managements, and on which the latter, because of the competitive character of the industry, have been forced to default. Nevertheless, as an explanation of the incidence of trade-union strength in the American economy, the theory of countervailing power clearly fits the broad contours of experience. There is, I venture, no other so satisfactory explanation of the great dynamic of labour organization in the modern capitalist community and none which so sensibly integrates the union into the theory of that society.

* It is important, as I have been reminded by the objections of English friends, to bear in mind that market power must always be viewed in relative terms. In the last century unions developed in the British textile industry and this industry in turn conformed broadly to the competition of the model. However, as buyers of labour the mill proprietors enjoyed a far stronger market position, the result of their greater resources and respect for their group interest, than did the individual workers.

The labour market serves admirably to illustrate the incentives to the development of countervailing power and it is of great importance in this market. However, its development, in response to positions of market power, is pervasive in the economy. As a regulatory device one of its most important manifestations is in the relation of the large retailer to the firms from which it buys. The way in which countervailing power operates in these markets is worth examining in some detail.

One of the seemingly harmless simplifications of formal economic theory has been the assumption that producers of consumers' goods sell their products directly to consumers. All business units are held, for this reason, to have broadly parallel interests. Each buys labour and materials, combines them and passes them along to the public at prices that, over some period of time, maximize returns. It is recognized that this is, indeed, a simplification; courses in marketing in the universities deal with what is excluded by this assumption. Yet it has long been supposed that the assumption does no appreciable violence to reality.

Did the real world correspond to the assumed one, the lot of the consumer would be an unhappy one. In fact goods pass to consumers by way of retailers and other intermediaries and this is a circumstance of first importance. Retailers are required by their situation to develop countervailing power on the consumer's behalf.

As I have previously observed, retailing remains one of the industries to which entry is characteristically free. It takes small capital and no very rare talent to set up as a seller of goods. Through history there have always been an ample supply of men with both and with access to something to sell. The small man can provide convenience and intimacy of service and can give an attention to detail, all of which allow him to co-exist with larger competitors.

The advantage of the larger competitor ordinarily lies in its lower prices. It lives constantly under the threat of an erosion of its business by the more rapid growth of rivals and by the appearance of new firms. This loss of volume, in turn, destroys the chance for the lower costs and lower prices on which the firm depends. This means that the larger retailer is extra-ordinarily sensitive to higher prices by its suppliers. It means also that it is strongly rewarded if it can develop the market power which permits it to force lower prices.

The opportunity to exercise such power exists only when the suppliers are enjoying something that can be taken away; i.e., when they are enjoying the fruits of market power from which they can be separated. Thus, as in the labour market, we find the mass retailer, from a position across the market with both a protective and a profit incentive to develop countervailing power when the firm with which it is doing business is in possession of market power. Critics have suggested that these are possibly important but certainly disparate phenomena. This may be so, but only if all similarity between social phenomena be denied. In the present instance the market context is the same. The motivating incentives are identical. The fact that it has characteristics in common has been what has caused people to call competition competition when they encountered it, say, in agriculture and then again in the laundry business.

Countervailing power in the retail business is identified with the large and powerful retail enterprises. Its practical mani-festation, over the last half-century, has been the rise of the food chains, the variety chains, the mail-order houses (now graduated into chain stores), the department-store chains, and the cooperative buying organizations of the surviving inde-pendent department and food stores.

This development was the countervailing response to previously established positions of power. The gains from invading these positions have been considerable and in some instances even spectacular. The rubber tyre industry is a fairly commonplace example of oligopoly. Four large firms are dominant in the market. In the thirties, Sears, Roebuck & Co. was able, by exploiting its role as a large and indispensable customer, to procure tyres from Goodyear Tyre & Rubber Company at a price from twenty-nine to forty per cent lower than the going market. These it resold to thrifty motorists for from a fifth to a quarter less than the same tyres carrying the regular Goodyear brand.

As a partial consequence of the failure of the government to recognize the role of countervailing power many hundreds of pages of court records have detailed the exercise of this power by the Great Atlantic & Pacific Tea Company. There is little doubt that this firm, at least in its uninhibited days, used the countervailing power it had developed with considerable artistry. In 1937, a survey by the company indicated that, for an investment of $175,000, it could supply itself with corn flakes. Assuming that it charged itself the price it was then paying to one of the three companies manufacturing this delicacy, it could earn a modest sixty-eight per cent on the outlay. Armed with this information, and the threat to go into the business which its power could readily make effective, it had no difficulty in bringing down the price by approximately ten per cent.* Such gains from the exercise of countervailing power, it will be clear, could only occur where there is an exercise of original market power with which to contend. The A & P could have reaped no comparable gains in buying staple products from the farmer. Committed as he is to the competition of the competitive model, the farmer has no gains to

* I am indebted to my friend Professor M. A. Adelman of the Massachusetts Institute of Technology for these details.

surrender. Provided, as he is, with the opportunity of selling all he produces at the impersonally determined market price, he has not the slightest incentive to make a special price to A & P at least beyond that which might in some circumstances be associated with the simple economies of bulk sale.

The examples of the exercise of countervailing power by Sears, Roebuck and A & P just cited show how this power is deployed in its most dramatic form. The day-to-day exercise of the buyer's power is a good deal less spectacular but also a good deal more significant. At the end of virtually every channel by which consumers' goods reach the public there is, in practice, a layer of powerful buyers. In the food market there are the great food chains; in clothing there are the department stores, the chain department stores, and the department store buying organizations; in appliances there are Sears, Roebuck and Montgomery Ward and the department stores; these latter firms are also important outlets for furniture and other house furnishings; the drug and cosmetic manufacturer has to seek part of his market through the large drug chains and the department stores; a vast miscellany of consumers' goods pass to the public through Woolworth's, Kresge's and other variety chains.

The buyers of all these firms deal directly with the manufacturer and there are few of the latter who, in setting prices, do not have to reckon with the attitude and reaction of their powerful customers. The retail buyers have a variety of weapons at their disposal to use against the market power of their suppliers. Their ultimate sanction is to develop their own source of supply as the food chains, Sears, Roebuck, and Montgomery Ward, have extensively done. They can also concentrate their entire patronage on a single supplier and, in return for a lower price, give him security in his volume and relieve him of selling and advertising costs. This policy has been widely followed and there have also been numerous complaints of the leverage it gives the retailer on his source of supply.

The more commonplace but more important tactic in the exercise of countervailing power consists, merely, in keeping the seller in a state of uncertainty as to the intentions of a buyer who is indispensable to him. The larger of the retail buying organizations place orders around which the production schedules and occasionally the investment of even the largest manufacturers become organized. A shift in this custom imposes prompt and heavy loss. The threat or even the fear of this sanction is enough to cause the supplier to surrender some or all of the rewards of his market power. He must frequently, in addition, make a partial surrender to less potent buyers if he is not to be more than ever in the power of his large customers. It will be clear that in this operation there are rare opportunities for playing one supplier off against another.

A measure of the importance which large retailing organizations attach to the deployment of their countervailing power is the prestige they accord to their buyers. These men (and women) are the key employees of the modern large retail organization; they are highly paid and they are among the most intelligent and resourceful people to be found anywhere in business. In the everyday course of business, they may be considerably better known and command rather more respect than the salesmen from whom they buy. This is a not unimportant index of the power they wield.

There are producers of consumers' goods who have protected themselves from exercise of countervailing power. Some, like the automobile and the oil industry, have done so by integrating their distribution through to the consumer – a strategy which attests the importance of the use of countervailing power by retailers. Others have found it possible to maintain dominance over an organization of small and dependent and therefore fairly powerless dealers. It seems probable that in a few industries, tobacco manufacture for example, the members are ordinarily strong enough and have sufficient solidarity to withstand any pressure applied to them by the most powerful buyer. However, even the tobacco manufacturers, under conditions that were especially favourable to the exercise of countervailing power in the thirties, were forced to make liberal price concessions, in the form of advertising allowances, to the A & P* and possibly also to other large customers. When the comprehensive representation of large retailers in the various fields of consumers' goods distribution is considered, it is reasonable to conclude – the reader is warned that this is an important generalization – that most positions of market power in the production of consumers' goods are covered by positions of countervailing power. As noted, there are exceptions and, as between markets, countervailing power is exercised with varying strength and effectiveness. The existence of exceptions does not impair the significance of the regulatory phenomenon here described. To its devotees the virtues of competition were great but few if any ever held its reign to be universal.

Countervailing power also manifests itself, although less visibly, in producers' goods markets. For many years the power of the automobile companies, as purchasers of steel, has sharply curbed the power of the steel mills as sellers. Detroit is the only city where the historic basing-point system was not used to price steel. Under the basing-point system, all producers regardless of location quoted the same price at any particular point of delivery. This obviously minimized the opportunity of a strong buyer to play one seller off against the other. The large firms in the automobile industry had developed the countervailing power which enabled them to do precisely this. They were not disposed to tolerate any limitations on their exercise of such power. In explaining the

* Richard B. Tennant, *The American Cigarette Industry* (New Haven: Yale University Press, 1950), p. 312.

quotation of 'arbitrary prices' on Detroit steel, a leading student of the basing-point system some years ago recognized, implicitly but accurately, the role of countervailing power by observing that 'it is difficult to apply high cartel prices to particularly large and strong customers such as the automobile manufacturers in Detroit.'*

The more normal operation of countervailing power in producers' goods markets has, as its point of departure, the relatively small number of customers which firms in these industries typically have. Where the cigarette or soap manufacturer numbers his retail outlets by the hundreds of thousands and his final consumers by the millions, the machinery or equipment manufacturer counts his customers by the hundreds or thousands and, very often, his important ones by the dozen. But here, as elsewhere, the market pays a premium to those who develop power as buyers that is equivalent to the market power of those from whom they buy. The reverse is true where weak sellers do business with strong buyers.

v

There is an old saying, or should be, that it is a wise economist who recognizes the scope of his own generalizations. It is now time to consider the limits in place and time on the operations of countervailing power. A study of the instances where countervailing power fails to function is not without advantage in showing its achievements in the decisively important areas where it does operate. As noted, some industries, because they are integrated through to the consumer or because their product passes through a dependent dealer organization, have not been faced with countervailing power. There are a few cases where a very strong market position has proven

* Fritz Machlup, *The Basing Point System* (Philadelphia: Blakiston Co., 1949), p. 115.

impregnable even against the attacks of strong buyers. And there are cases where the dangers from countervailing power have, apparently, been recognized and where it has been successfully resisted.

An example of successful resistance to countervailing power is the residential-building industry. No segment of American capitalism evokes less pride. Yet anyone approaching the industry with the preconceptions of competition in mind is unlikely to see, very accurately, the reasons for its short-comings. There are many thousands of individual firms in the business of building houses. Nearly all are small; the capital of the typical housebuilder runs from a few hundred to a few thousand dollars. The members of the industry oppose little market power to the would-be house owner. Except in times of extremely high building activity there is aggressive competition for business.

The industry does show many detailed manifestations of guild restraint. Builders are frequently in alliance with each other, unions, and local politicians to protect prices and wages and to maintain established building techniques. These dere-lictions have been seized upon avidly by the critics of the industry. Since they represent its major departure from the competitive model, they have been assumed to be the cause of the poor performance of the housing industry. It has long been an article of faith with liberals that if competition could be brought to the housing business all would be well.

In fact were all restraint and collusion swept away – were there full and free competition in bidding, no restrictive building codes, no collusion with union leaders or local politi-cians to enhance prices – it seems improbable that the price of new houses would be much changed and the satisfaction of customers with what they get for what they pay much enhanced. The reason is that the typical builder would still be a small and powerless figure buying his building materials in small quantities at high cost from suppliers with effective market power and facing in this case essentially the same problem *vis-à-vis* the unions as sellers of labour. It is these factors which, very largely, determine the cost of the house.

The builder is more or less deliberately kept without power. With few exceptions, the manufacturers of building supplies decline to sell to him direct. This prevents any builder from bringing pressure to bear on his source of supply; at the same time it helps keep all builders relatively small and powerless by uniformly denying them the economies of direct purchase. All must pay jobbers' and retailers' margins. A few builders – a spectacular case is Levitt & Sons of Long Island – have managed to circumvent this ban.* As the result of more effective buying, a much stronger position in dealing with labour, and the savings from large-scale production of houses, they have notably increased the satisfaction of customers with what they receive for their money. Few can doubt that the future of the industry, if its future is to improve on its past, lies with such firms.

Thus it is the notion of countervailing power, not of competition, which points the way to progress in the housing industry. What is needed is fewer firms of far greater scale with resulting capacity to bring power to bear upon unions and suppliers. It is the absence of such firms, and of the resulting economies, which helps explain why one sector of this industry – low-cost housing where cost is especially important in relation to ability-to-pay – has passed under government management. In the absence of an effective regulating mechanism within the industry in the form of countervailing power, private entrepreneurship has been superseded. In accordance

* Levitt has established a wholly owned building-supply company to buy materials for its projects. *Fortune*, August 1947, p. 168. He also, most significantly, grew to importance as a non-union employer.

with classical expectations the state has had to intervene. Only the failure was not of competition but of countervailing power.

## VI

The development of countervailing power requires a certain minimum opportunity and capacity for organization, corporate or otherwise. If the large retail buying organizations had not developed the countervailing power which they have used, by proxy, on behalf of the individual consumer, consumers would have been faced with the need to organize the equivalent of the retailer's power. This would have been a formidable task but it has been accomplished in Scandinavia where the consumer's cooperative, instead of the chain store, is the dominant instrument of countervailing power in consumers' goods markets. There has been a similar though less comprehensive development in England and Scotland. In the Scandinavian countries the cooperatives have long been regarded explicitly as instruments for bringing power to bear on the cartels; i.e., for exercise of countervailing power. This is readily conceded by many who have the greatest difficulty in seeing private mass buyers in the same role. But the fact that consumer cooperatives are not of any great importance in the United States is to be explained, not by any inherent incapacity of the American for such organization, but because the chain stores pre-empted the gains of countervailing power first. The counterpart of the Swedish Kooperative Forbundet or the British Co-operative Wholesale Societies has not appeared in the United States simply because it could not compete with the A & P and other large food chains. The meaning of this, which incidentally has been lost on devotees of the theology of cooperation, is that the chain stores are approximately as efficient in the exercise of countervailing power as a cooperative would be. In parts of the American economy where proprietary mass buyers have not made their appearance, notably in the purchase of farm supplies, individuals (who are also individualists) have shown as much capacity to organize as the Scandinavians and the British and have similarly obtained the protection and rewards of countervailing power. The Grange League Federation, the Eastern States Farmers' Exchange, and the Illinois Farm Supply Company, cooperatives with annual sales running to multi-million-dollar figures, are among the illustrations of the point.

However, it must not be assumed that it is easy for great numbers of individuals to coalesce and organize countervailing power. In less developed communities, Puerto Rico for example, one finds people fully exposed to the exactions of strategically situated importers, merchants, and wholesalers and without the apparent capacity to develop countervailing power in their own behalf. Anyone, incidentally, who doubts the force of the countervailing power exercised by large retailer-buying organizations would do well to consider the revolution which the entry of the large chain stores would work in an economy like that of Puerto Rico and also how such an intrusion would be resented and perhaps resisted by importers and merchants now able to exercise their market power with impunity against the thousands of small, independent, and inefficient retailers who are their present outlets.*

In the light of the difficulty in organizing countervailing power, it is not surprising that the assistance of government has repeatedly been sought in this task. Without the phenomenon itself being fully recognized, the provision of state assistance to the development of countervailing power has become a major function of government – perhaps *the* major domestic function of government. Much of the domestic legislation of the last twenty years, that of the New Deal

---

* This is the subject of a detailed study recently published by the Harvard University Press. (*Marketing Efficiency in Puerto Rico* by John Kenneth Galbraith, Richard H. Holton, and colleagues.)

episode in particular, only becomes fully comprehensible when it is viewed in this light. To this I shall return in the next chapter.

## VII

I come now to the major limitation on the operation of countervailing power – a matter of much importance in our time. Countervailing power is not exercised uniformly under all conditions of demand. It does not function at all as a restraint on market power when there is inflation or inflationary pressure on markets.

Because the competitive model, in association with Say's Law, was assumed to find its equilibrium at or near full employment levels, economists for a long time were little inclined to inquire whether markets in general, or competition in particular, might behave differently at different levels of economic activity, i.e., whether they might behave differently in prosperity and depression. In any case the conventional division of labour in economics has assigned to one group of scholars the task of examining markets and competitive behaviour, to another a consideration of the causes of fluctuations in the economy. The two fields of exploration are even today separated by watertight bulkheads, or less metaphorically, by professorial division of labour and course requirements. Those who have taught and written on market behaviour have assumed a condition of general stability in the economy in which sellers were eager for buyers. To the extent, as on occasion in recent years, that they have had to do their teaching or thinking in a time of inflation – in a time when, as the result of strong demand, eager buyers were besieging reluctant sellers – they have dismissed the circumstance as abnormal. They have drawn their classroom and textbook illustrations from the last period of deflation, severe or mild.

So long as competition was assumed to be the basic regulatory force in the economy these simplifications, although they led to some error, were not too serious. There is a broad continuity in competitive behaviour from conditions of weak to conditions of strong demand. At any given moment there is a going price in competitive markets that reflects the current equilibrium of supply-and-demand relationships. Even though demand is strong and prices are high and rising, the seller who prices above the going or equilibrium level is punished by the loss of his customers. The buyer still has an incentive to look for the lowest price he can find. Thus market behaviour is not fundamentally different from what it is when demand is low and prices are falling.

There are, by contrast, differences of considerable importance in market behaviour between conditions of insufficient and excessive demand when there is oligopoly, i.e., when the market has only a small number of sellers. The convention against price competition, when small numbers of sellers share a market, is obviously not very difficult to maintain if all can sell all they produce and none is subject to the temptation to cut prices. Devices like price leadership, open book pricing, and the basing-point system which facilitate observance of the convention all work well because they are under little strain. Thus the basing-point system by making known, or easily calculable, the approved prices at every possible point of delivery in the country provided protection against accidental or surreptitious price-cutting. Such protection is not necessary when there is no temptation to cut prices. By an interesting paradox when the basing-point system was attacked by the government in the late depression years it was of great consequence to the steel, cement, and other industries that employed it. When, after the deliberate processes of the law, the system was finally abolished by the courts in April 1948, the consequences for the industries in question were rather slight. The steel and cement companies were then straining to meet demand that was in excess of their capacity. They were under no temptation to cut prices and thus had no current reason to regret the passing of the basing-point system.

These differences in market behaviour under conditions of strong and of weak demand are important and there are serious grounds for criticizing their neglect – or rather the assumption that there is normally a shortage of buyers – in the conventional market analysis. However, the effect of changes in demand on market behaviour becomes of really profound significance only when the role of countervailing power is recognized.

Countervailing power, as fully noted in the earlier parts of this chapter, is organized either by buyers or by sellers in response to a stronger position across the market. But strength, i.e., relative strength, obviously depends on the state of aggregate demand. When demand is strong, especially when it is at inflationary levels, the bargaining position of poorly organized or even of unorganized workers is favourable. When demand is weak the bargaining position of the strongest union deteriorates to some extent. The situation is similar where countervailing power is exercised by a buyer. A scarcity of demand is a prerequisite to his bringing power to bear on suppliers. If buyers are plentiful – if supply is small in relation to current demand – sellers are under no compulsion to surrender to the bargaining power of any particular customer. They have alternatives.\*

\* The everyday business distinction between a 'buyers' and a 'sellers' market and the frequency of its use reflect the importance which participants in actual markets attach to the ebb and flow of countervailing power. That this distinction has no standing in formal economics follows from the fact that countervailing power has not been recognized by economists. As frequently happens, practical men have devised a terminology to denote a phenomenon of great significance to themselves but which, since it has not been assimilated to economic theory, has never appeared in the textbooks. The concept of the 'break-even point', generally employed by businessmen but largely ignored in economic theory, is another case in point.

Broadly speaking, positions of countervailing power have been developed in a context of limited – or, more accurately, of not unlimited – demand. This is partly because such periods have had a much higher incidence in history than the episodes of unlimited or inflationary demand. It is partly because periods of drastically restricted demand, by providing exceptional opportunity for aggression by the strong against the weak, have also provided an exceptional incentive to building countervailing power. Much of the structure of organization on which countervailing power depends traces its origins to such periods.

The depression years of the thirties, needless to say, were a particularly fruitful period in this respect. Accordingly, and in sharp contrast with most other types of business, these years were very favourable to the development of the chain stores and also of various group buying enterprises. The intensity of the trade agitation against the mass retailers, culminating in 1936 in the passage of the Robinson-Patman Act (designed as we shall see presently to limit their exercise of this power), was itself a measure of the chain's advantage in this period. By contrast, during the years of strong demand and short supply of the Second World War, the chain stores lost ground, relatively, to independents. As this strong demand in relation to supply destroyed their capacity to exercise countervailing power, their advantage disappeared. It is likewise interesting to note that the trade agitation and resentment against the chains almost completely disappeared during the war and post-war years.

The depression years also provided a notable inducement to the trade union movement. With prosperity in the forties and fifties, labour organization too lost its momentum. Finally, to the depression years we owe nearly all of the modern arrangements for exercise of countervailing power by and on behalf of the farmers.

Given this structural accommodation by the economy to limited demand, the appearance of unlimited demand is somewhat devastating. There is everywhere a shift of bargaining power to sellers. The balance of force appropriate to limited demand is everywhere upset. The market power of strong sellers, until now offset by that of strong buyers, is enhanced. The countervailing power of weak sellers is suddenly and adventitiously reinforced.

These effects can again be seen with greatest clarity in the labour market. Here they also have their most portentous consequences. In industries where strong firms bargain with strong unions, the management of the former has what has come to be considered a normal resistance to wage increases when demand is not pressing upon capacity. To yield is to increase unit costs. The firm cannot with impunity pass along these higher costs to its customers. There may be a question as to whether other firms in the industry will follow suit; there will always be a question of the effect of the higher prices on sales. If the demand for the products is in any measure elastic the consequence of the higher prices will be a loss of volume. This, with its effect on employment in the industry, is something of which modern union leadership, as well as management, is usually conscious. Thus the trial of strength between union and management associated with collective bargaining is, essentially although not exclusively, over the division of profits. When demand is limited, we have, in other words, an essentially healthy manifestation of countervailing power. The union opposes its power as a seller of labour to that of management as a buyer: principally at stake is the division of the returns. An occasional strike is an indication that countervailing power is being employed in a sound context where the costs of any wage increase cannot readily be passed along to someone else. It should be an occasion for mild rejoicing in the conservative press. The *Daily Worker*, eagerly contemplating the downfall of capitalism, should regret this manifestation of the continued health of the system.

Under conditions of strong demand, however, collective bargaining takes on a radically different form. Then management is no longer constrained to resist union demands on the grounds that higher prices will be reflected in shrinking volume. There is now an adequate supply of eager buyers. The firm that first surrenders to the union need not worry lest it be either the first or the only one to increase prices. There are buyers for all. No one has occasion, as the result of price increases, to worry about a general shrinkage in volume. A strong demand means an inelastic demand. On the other hand, there are grave disadvantages for management in resisting the union. Since profits are not at stake, any time lost as the result of a strike is a dead loss. Worker morale and the actual loss of part of the working force to employers who offer better wages must be reckoned with. Thus when demand is sufficiently strong to press upon the capacity of industry generally to supply it, there is no real conflict of interest between union and employer. Or to put it differently, all bargaining strength shifts to the side of the union. The latter becomes simply an engine for increasing prices, for it is to the mutual advantage of union and employer to effect a coalition and to pass the costs of their agreement on in higher prices. Other buyers along the line, who under other circumstances might have exercised their countervailing power against the price increases, are similarly inhibited. Thus under inflationary pressure of demand, the whole structure of countervailing power in the economy is dissolved.

We were able to witness one fairly good example of this dissolution of countervailing power in the continuing rounds of wage and price increases following the Second World War. The full coalition between management and labour, under the conditions of inflationary demand of these years, was partly disguised by the conventional expressions of animosity and by the uncertainty of management as to how long the inflation would last. However, by 1950–1 the 'Fifth Round' was negotiated with scarcely an important strike. The President of the United States Steel Corporation, in yielding to the union in November 1950, indicated a *de facto* coalition when he pointed out that the 'half-cent' inflation in steel prices, which would be passed along to customers, was a small price to pay for 'uninterrupted and expanded' production. The consequences of this failure of countervailing power in times of inflation are considerable. They take on added importance with the easing of the depression psychosis with the passage of years. I shall return to these problems in the final chapter. First, however, it is necessary to examine the role of the state in the development of countervailing power.

# CHAPTER 10

# Countervailing Power and the State

I

IN their relations with government, the American people have long shown a considerable ability to temper doctrine by pragmatism. The ruggedly conservative businessman who excoriates Statism, the Welfare State, and the State Department has never allowed his convictions to interfere with an approach to the government for a tariff if he really needs it. The impeccably conservative business journal which editorially condemns Keynesians and deficit spending as heralds of disaster does not fail to point out on the financial page that the effect of the deficit in the new budget, which it so deplores, will be favourable to business volume and earnings. The up-country cotton or tobacco planter whose belief in States' rights is unequalled except by his mistrust of civil rights votes, none the less, for federally administered marketing quotas, tolerates a remarkably comprehensive form of agricultural regimentation.

Since the phenomenon of countervailing power is of much practical importance, even though it for long went unrecognized in economic and political theory, we should expect, in line with our highly pragmatic approach to government, that it would have been the object of a good deal of legislation and the subject of a good deal of government policy. As the last chapter has made clear, there are strong incentives in the modern economy for developing countervailing power. Moreover, the group that seeks countervailing power is, initially, a numerous and disadvantaged group which seeks organization because it faces, in its market, a much smaller and much more advantaged group. This situation is well calculated to excite public sympathy and, because there are numerous votes involved, to recruit political support.

In fact, the support of countervailing power has become in modern times perhaps the major domestic peacetime function of the federal government. Labour sought and received it in the protection and assistance which the Wagner Act provided to union organization. Farmers sought and received it in the form of federal price supports to their markets – a direct subsidy of market power. Unorganized workers have sought and received it in the form of minimum wage legislation. The bituminous-coal mines sought and received it in the Bituminous Coal Conservation Act of 1935 and the National Bituminous Coal Act of 1937.* These measures, all designed to give a group a market power it did not have before, comprised the most important legislative acts of the New Deal. They fuelled the sharpest domestic controversies of the New and Fair Deals.

There should be no problem as to why this legislation, and the administrations that sponsored it, were keenly controversial. The groups that sought the assistance of government in building countervailing power sought that power in order to use it against market authority to which they had previously been subordinate. Those whose power was thereby inhibited could hardly be expected to welcome this development or the intervention of the government to abet it.

Because the nature of countervailing power has not been firmly grasped, the government's role in relation to it has not only been imperfectly understood but also imperfectly played. One is permitted to hope that a better understanding of

---

* The first Act was declared unconstitutional in 1936; the second was allowed to expire during the war when an excess of demand had more than adequately reinforced the bargaining power of the mine operators.

countervailing power will contribute to better administration in the future.

## II

The role of countervailing power in the economy marks out two broad problems in policy for the government. In all but conditions of inflationary demand, countervailing power performs a valuable – indeed an indispensable – regulatory function in the modern economy. Accordingly it is incumbent upon government to give it freedom to develop and to determine how it may best do so. The government also faces the question of where and how it will affirmatively support the development of countervailing power. It will be convenient to look first at the negative role of the government in allowing the development of countervailing power and then to consider its affirmative role in promoting it.

At the outset a somewhat general distinction – one that is implicit in the discussion of the last chapter – must be made between countervailing and original power.* When, anywhere in the course of producing, processing, or distributing a particular product, one or a few firms first succeed in establishing a strong market position they may be considered to be the possessors of original market power. They are able, as the result of their power over the prices they pay or charge, to obtain more than normal margins and profits.† These are at the expense of the weaker suppliers or customers. This is the monopoly position anciently feared by liberals and as anciently condemned by economists, and their instincts were sound.

---

\* William J. Fellner in his book, *Competition among the Few: Oligopoly and Similar Market Structures* (New York: Alfred A. Knopf Co., 1949), observes that the market power of unions, in relation to that of corporations, is of a neutralizing not an additive character. It will be evident, I think, that this involves a distinction to the one I am making.

† Technically prices or margins in excess of marginal costs.

Countervailing power invades such positions of strength, whether they be held by suppliers or customers, and redresses the position of the weaker group.

The rule to be followed by government is, in principle, a clear one. There can be very good reason for attacking positions of original market power in the economy if these are not effectively offset by countervailing power. There is at least a theoretical justification for opposing all positions of market power. There is no justification for attacking positions of countervailing power which leaves positions of original market power untouched. On the contrary, damage both in equity and to the most efficient operation of the economy will be the normal consequence of doing so.

The problems of practical application of such a rule are mostly in the field of the antitrust laws and they are a good deal more difficult than the simple articulation of the rule implies. However a general distinction between original and countervailing power is, in fact, now made in the antitrust laws – it has been forced, against the accepted current of ideas concerning competition, by the practical reality of the phenomenon itself.

In the first development of positions of market power, a long lead was assumed by the capitalist industrial enterprise. The formidable structure of Marxian socialism was based on the assumption that this power was great and, short of revolution, immutable. As a broad historical fact such enterprise is the *locus* of original market power. When workers and farmers sought to develop strength in the sale of their labour power and products, they did so in markets where industrial firms had already achieved positions of original power. It would be broadly in harmony with the distinction between original and countervailing power to exclude labour and farm organizations from prosecution under the antitrust laws. This has been done. While the Sherman Act made no mention of labour, Congress did not have in mind the still modest efforts of unions to lift their bargaining power when it enacted the legislation of 1890. Subsequently, unions became subject to the law by judicial interpretation. Indeed, in the first few decades that the legislation was in effect, unions were a primary target. This led to their exclusion by name in the Clayton Act of 1914. After the Supreme Court had somewhat obdurately reincluded them in 1921 (Justices Brandeis, Holmes, and Clarke dissenting) they were again and finally excluded by the Norris-LaGuardia Act of 1932 and by the subsequent and more benign decisions of a New Deal Court.

Similarly, efforts by farm cooperatives to enhance the market power of the farmer, so long as they are held within reason, are excluded by the Clayton Act of 1914, by further legislation (the Capper-Volstead Act) in 1922 and in more specific instances by the Agricultural Marketing Agreement Act of 1937. Congress has thus recognized, implicitly, that the efforts of labour and agriculture to develop market power were different from those of industrial firms. The difference – the by now plausible difference – was that these efforts were the response of workers and farmers to the power of those to whom they sold their labour or products.

A more precise and conscious use of the distinction between original and countervailing power would take account of the fact that some trade unions and some farm groups are clearly the possessors of original power. Thus workers in the building trades, although they are not highly organized or exceptionally powerful in any absolute sense, are strong in relation to the small-scale employers with whom they do business. They are clearly the possessors of original market power. The special nature of their power, as compared with that of the trade-union movement generally, explains the distress of men and women who have reacted sympathetically to the role of unions in general but who, in this uncomfortable case, have found themselves on the side of organizations that have plenary power to restrict output and enhance their own income. The obvious answer to the problem lies in the distinction between original and countervailing power. This, logically, would make restrictive practices of master plumbers or plasterers a proper object of interest by the Department of Justice while the absolutely (though not relatively) far more powerful unions in steel or automobiles who impose no similar restrictions on the supply of their labour would not be.*

Similarly, there are undoubted cases of exercise of original power by groups of agricultural producers. The immunity granted by existing laws is not complete – the Secretary of Agriculture is authorized to enter a complaint if, as a result of the activities of the cooperative, prices are 'unduly enhanced', and a cooperative cannot merge its power with non-agricultural corporations. As a result there have been a scattering of prosecutions of farmers' organizations – of the former California Fruit Growers' Exchange (Sunkist oranges) and of a Chicago milkshed producers' organization which was charged with being in combination in restraint of trade with milk distributors, unions, and even a college professor. But such cases have been infrequent.

However, the more serious consequences of the failure to perceive the role of countervailing power have been within the fabric of industry itself. The antitrust laws have been indiscriminately invoked against firms that have succeeded in building countervailing power, while holders of original market power, against whom the countervailing power was developed, have gone unchallenged. Such action has placed the authority of law on the side of positions of monopoly power and against

* Again, government policy has shown a tendency to recognize, pragmatically, distinctions which are not recognized in the available theory. In 1940 the original power of the building trades unions was attacked by the Department of Justice. However, by eventual decision of the Supreme Court – *U.S.* v. *Hutcheson et al.*, 312 U.S. 219 (1940) – the unions were held to be substantially immune.

the interests of the public at large. The effects have been damaging to the economy and also to the prestige of the anti-trust laws.

### III

As the last chapter has made clear, one of the most important instruments for exercise of countervailing power is the large retail organization. These by proxy are the public's main line of defence against the market power of those who produce or process consumers' goods. We have seen that they are an American counterpart of the consumer cooperatives which, in other countries, are viewed explicitly as an instrument for countering the power of the cartels. Yet the position of the large retail organizations has been not only a general, but also in some measure a unique, object of government attack. Chain stores and other large buyers have been frequent recent objects of Sherman Act prosecution and are the special target of the Robinson-Patman Act which is especially designed to inhibit their exercise of countervailing power.

Under the provisions of the Robinson-Patman Act a chain store may receive the benefit of the demonstrably lower costs of filling the large orders which it places; it may not receive concessions that are the result of its superior bargaining power. The effect, since these concessions are important only when won from positions of original economic power, is to discriminate in favour of original power and against countervailing power.

The effects of failure to distinguish between original and countervailing power have been especially noteworthy in the several suits against the Great Atlantic and Pacific Tea Company. This company was prosecuted before the war for violation of the Robinson-Patman Act,* was convicted of violation of the Sherman Act in a case brought in 1944 and finally

* *Great Atlantic & Pacific Tea Co.* v. *FTC*, 106 F. 2d 667 (1939).

decided in 1949,* and was thereafter, for a period, again a defendant. In spite of its many legal misadventures, the company has not been charged with, or even seriously suspected of, exploiting the consumer. On the contrary, its crime has been too vigorous bargaining, which bargaining was, effectively, on the consumer's behalf. In the case brought in 1944 it was charged with seeking to increase its volume by reducing its margins and with bringing its bargaining power too vigorously to bear upon its suppliers in order to get price reductions. These suppliers – which included such powerful sellers as the large canning companies – had long been involved in a trial of strength with A & P over prices. They were left undisturbed. The government was in the highly equivocal position of prosecuting activities which have the effect of keeping down prices to the consumer. The positions of market power, which had given A & P its opportunity, were left untouched.

The litigation against A & P was strongly defended. Although the firm did rather less than ten per cent of the food-retailing business, had strong rivals, and was in an industry where, as observed in the last chapter, the entry of new firms is singularly easy, the danger was much stressed that it might achieve an effective monopoly of food-retailing. Nevertheless one can hardly doubt that these cases were a source of serious embarrassment to friends of the antitrust laws. No explanation, however elaborate, could quite conceal the fact that the effect of antitrust enforcement, in this case, was to the disadvantage of the public. Viewed in light of the present analysis the reason becomes evident. The prosecution, by inhibiting the exercise of countervailing power, provided protection to the

* *U.S.* v. *New York Great Atlantic & Pacific Tea Co.*, 67 F. Supplement 626 (1946). For a discussion of this case see M. A. Adelman, 'The A & P Case: A Study in Applied Economic Theory', *Quarterly Journal of Economics* (May 1949), pp. 238ff.

very positions of market power that are anathema to the defender of the antitrust laws.*

No one should conclude, from the foregoing, that an exemption of countervailing power should now be written into the antitrust laws. A considerable gap has always separated useful economic concepts from applicable legal ones. However, a number of conclusions, with immediate bearing on the antitrust laws, do follow from this analysis. In the first place the mere possession and exercise of market power is not a useful criterion for antitrust action. The further and very practical question must be asked: Against whom and for what purposes is the power being exercised? Unless this question is asked and the answer makes clear that the public is the victim, the antitrust laws, by attacking countervailing power, can as well enhance as reduce monopoly power.

Secondly, it is clear that some damage can be done to the economy by such legislation as the Robinson-Patman Act. This legislation is the culmination of a long and confused legal and legislative struggle dating from 1914 over what economists have come to call price discrimination. The

---

* Much of the pressure for the Robinson-Patman Act and its enforcement (and in lesser measure also the State Fair Trade laws which have a similar ultimate effect) came and continues to come from the smaller competitors of the chains who do not themselves have effective countervailing power. They have, in effect, sought to protect their own weaker buying position by denying strength to others. This is wholly understandable but it has not been the only recourse of the independent. He has had the alternative of joining his bargaining power, as a buyer, with other independents. And, in some fields – food-retailing and department stores for example – such cooperative bargaining has enjoyed a large measure of success. A clearer view of original and countervailing power by public authority would also have made this the preferred way of protecting the position of the independent retailer. In short, the public would have been better served by a more comprehensive development of countervailing power by retailers than by a policy which sought to eliminate the advantages associated with its possession by denying it to all.

ostensible motive of the legislation is to protect competition. The seller is prevented from giving a lower price to one customer than to another where the lower price cannot be justified by the economies associated with the particular sale and where the effect is 'to injure, destroy, or prevent' competition either with the seller or between his customers. The practical effect, reinforced by recent court decisions, is to make any important price concessions to any large buyer of questionable legality.*

Even those who are unwavering in their belief in competition have been inclined to doubt whether this legislation does much to protect competition. What is not doubtful at all is that the legislation strikes directly at the effective exercise of countervailing power. To achieve price discrimination – to use bargaining power to get a differentially lower price – is the very essence of the exercise of countervailing power. In trying, with questionable effect, to preserve one of the autonomous regulators of the economy the government is seriously impairing another.

Finally, the theory of countervailing power throws important light on the advantage of different numbers of firms in an industry and on the objectives of the antitrust laws in relation thereto. One of the effects of the new ideas on market theory, as noted in Chapter 4, was to raise serious doubts whether an industry of small numbers was, in fact, socially preferable to a monopoly. Once firms had recognized their interdependence, it was believed that they would find a price, output, and profit position not greatly different from that which would be achieved by a single firm. This made it

* Especially *FTC* v. *Morton Salt Company*, 334 U.S. 37 (1948) although a still more recent decision makes legitimate concessions to meet the price of another seller (*Standard Oil of Indiana* v. *FTC* 71 S. Ct. 240, 1951).

doubtful whether it was worth while to prosecute a monopoly in order to create an oligopoly.

The examination of the relation of oligopoly to technical change and development will already have raised some questions about this conclusion. There is reason to suppose that an industry characterized by oligopoly will be more progressive than an industry controlled by one firm. Recognition of the role of countervailing power suggests a further clear advantage on the side of the oligopoly. One can hardly doubt that, in general, it will be much easier for countervailing power to break into a position of market strength maintained by an imperfect coalition of three, four, or a dozen firms than into a position held by one firm. When there is more than one firm in a market there are opportunities for playing one off against another. Mistrust and uncertainty can be developed in the mind of one *entrepreneur* as to the intentions and good faith of others. These, in turn, can be translated into bargaining concessions. Such opportunities abruptly disappear when the number is reduced to one.

Thus the theory of countervailing power comes to the defence of the antitrust laws at what has been a very vulnerable point. Efforts to prevent or to disperse single-firm control of an industry can be defended for the greater opening they provide for the exercise of countervailing power. Similar and equally good reasons exist for resisting mergers. Those who have always believed there was something uniquely evil about monopoly are at least partly redeemed by the theory of countervailing power.

IV

It must surely be agreed that, during the present century, American economic and political life have gained in strength as the result of the improved position of workers and farmers – two important and once disadvantaged groups. A scant fifty years ago American labour relations were characterized by sullenness, anger, and fear. Farmer attitudes were marked by a deep sense of insecurity and inferiority. There can be little question that these attitudes were an aspect of economic inferiority. Workers and farmers lived in the knowledge that they were subject, in one way or another, to the power of others. It was inevitable, therefore, that with the development of countervailing power these attitudes would change and they have. In place of the inferiority and insecurity has come a well-developed sense of equality and confidence. It would seem difficult, indeed, to argue that the American economy and polity is anything but stronger as a result.

That argument has been made – and vigorously since this book first appeared. Social serenity would seem to be a plausible social goal. It would seem to the common advantage that there be, at any given time, no open or suppressed revolution. However, change and innovation which have as their main purpose the relief of social tension do not have much standing in economics, at least with those whose eyes are trained on the competitive model as a social norm. There are some who would accept a little turbulence in pursuit of so admirable a goal. For others this is not a matter for the economists to worry about. They can watch the rioting from the window.

In this tradition, the sufficient and only test of social change is whether, assuming organization and technology to be given, it reduces prices to the consumer. This is not a test which countervailing power can always satisfy. The development of such power by workers or farmers may result primarily in a redistribution of returns. It may, by raising marginal costs, raise prices to the consumer.

However, apart from the error in the purely static character of this test, it is evident that it is socially limited to the point of being frivolous. The political attitudes of those who are subject to economic power are rarely benign. In numerous lands at numerous times they have been violently the reverse. Obviously the elimination of these tensions is no less a goal because it has a price. It remains to add that there is no indication that the price has ever been considerable.

A number who have accepted as desirable the development of countervailing power by previously disadvantaged groups have been none the less careful to point out that it is decidedly a second-best solution. Given the power of the modern industrial corporation, it is doubtless well that those who do business with it have the capacity to protect themselves. But how much better to have avoided this struggle between the behemoths. There is something frightening and possibly dangerous about this bargaining between vast aggregations. How much better to have denied power to all. The world of countervailing power may be tolerable but it is highly imperfect.

This is an appealing argument although it is not likely to appeal to anyone who is interested in results. Past efforts to extirpate economic power have been notably unavailing. One cannot suppose that they will be more successful in the future. Economic power may indeed be inherent in successful capitalism. We had better be content with restraints we have than to search for a never-never land in which they would be rendered unnecessary.

Finally, there has been special concern over the role which government has played in the development of countervailing power. As noted, farmers, workers, and numerous other groups have sought and received government assistance, either in the form of direct support to their market power or in support to organization which in turn made market power possible. In short, the government has subsidized with its own power the countervailing power of workers, farmers, and others. (The efforts on behalf of agriculture reveal so many facets of the problem of countervailing power that they are worth examining in some detail. This is done in the next chapter.) This assistance, clearly, explains some part of the self-confidence and well-being which these groups display today.

Yet few courses of policy have ever been undertaken more grudgingly and with a greater sense of guilt. One can scarcely imagine a government action which, on the record, has produced more beneficent results in practice in which less pride has been taken. Especially in the case of agriculture, all measures have, until recently, been characterized as 'emergency' legislation. This is invariably our label for excusing to our consciences action which seems to be at once wise and unwise.

The principal reason for this sense of guilt, no doubt, is that the notion of a government subsidy of its power to groups seeking to develop countervailing power has never enjoyed a place in the accredited structure of American economic and political science. Accordingly the unfinished tasks of developing such power have never had a place on the reformer's calendar. The reformer, in fact, has almost invariably been overtaken by the action. When the groups in question have developed enough influence to obtain government assistance on their own behalf they have simply gone ahead and got it without blessing or benefit of doctrine. As the role of countervailing power comes to be understood, we can expect that much of the anxiety that is evoked by government support to the process will disappear.

We shall also view with more equanimity the extension of countervailing power in the economy. What has strengthened the American economy so admirably in the past must be presumed to have an unexploited potential for good in the future.

There are still some millions of Americans who are without any organized expression of market power and whose standards of living and welfare are categorical evidence of the consequences. These include, for example, some two million hired farm workers, the truly forgotten men of American life. They have no security in their employment – there are few that cannot be fired on a day's notice. They have only limited social security benefits; they are normally unprotected by workmen's compensation in what is a fairly hazardous occupation; many do not have a fixed place of abode; their pay, even in times when there is a strong demand for their services, is far from handsome. A share in the gains from the newly developed market power of the farmer has still to be transmitted to his hired man.

There are also the unorganized urban workers, those on the fringes of the labour movement and, perhaps most important of all, occupational categories which, in the past, have foresworn efforts to develop economic power. Schoolteachers, clerical workers, municipal employees, and civil servants have generally avoided organization as something not quite genteel or because it was believed that employers and the community at large would recognize their importance and pay accordingly. In addition the natural leaders among white-collar workers have had, as ordinary workers had not, the clear alternative of obtaining promotion. A ten per cent increase in pay is not of great consequence to a high-school mathematics teacher if he is soon to become principal. This self-denying ordinance by white-collar workers where organization is concerned has invariably been viewed with approval, even as a manifestation of patriotism and sound Americanism, by public authorities and private employers.

Quite possibly the white-collar groups did not suffer too severely from their lack of market power in the years before the Second World War. In times of stable prices the salaried worker seeks an increase in pay only for the sake of increasing his real income. His weakness is not likely – as with the wage earner contending against pay cuts – to cost him ground. A skilful negotiator can do much for himself.\* However, in times of rising prices, market power must be exercised affirmatively if past positions are to be held. It seems to me possible that the next group to seek to assert its market power will be the genteel white-collar class. In any case, we cannot assume that efforts by presently unorganized groups to seek market power, and to seek the assistance of government in their effort, is finished business.

In the actual sequence of events, some measure of organization by the group themselves must precede any very important government subsidy to their developing market power. Not until farmers and workers achieved some organization on their own behalf were they able to get the state to reinforce their efforts. In the thirties the Farm Security Administration, an idealistic and imaginative effort to help subsistence and tenant farmers and farm workers, largely petered out because those aided lacked the organization to defend in Congress and before the public the efforts being made on their behalf. Support to countervailing power is not endowed, *ad hoc*, by government. It must be sought.

v

At this point it becomes possible to answer, at least tentatively, one of the questions with which this essay was launched. That is the meaning of the great expansion of state activity

---

\* Though clearly this is not a simple business. The psychological crisis of the devoted but unassertive white-collar employee when he must appeal for a salary raise is one of the most reliable topics of the American cartoonist. The popularity of the theme, apart from revealing the intransigent sadism of cartoonists and their audience, suggests that the problem depicted is a real one.

in recent decades, the expansion which conservatives have found so alarming and which many liberals have supported without knowing quite why. We can now see that a large part of the state's new activity – the farm legislation, labour legislation, minimum-wage legislation – is associated with the development of countervailing power. As such it is neither adventitious nor abnormal; the government action supports or supplements a normal economic process. Steps to strengthen countervailing power are not, in principle, different from steps to strengthen competition. Given the existence of private market power in the economy, the growth of counter-vailing power strengthens the capacity of the economy for autonomous self-regulation and thereby lessens the amount of over-all government control or planning that is required or sought.

Two or three further points may be made. Increasingly, in our time, we may expect domestic political differences to turn on the question of supporting or not supporting efforts to develop countervailing power. Liberalism will be identi-fied with the buttressing of weak bargaining positions in the economy; conservatism – and this may well be its proper function – will be identified with the protection of positions of original power. There will be debate over whether weak positions have been unduly strengthened. The struggle over the Taft-Hartley Act is an example of the kind of political issue which countervailing power can be expected to develop. The essential question at issue in the Taft-Hartley contro-versy was whether, in the process of buttressing a weak bargaining position, the government had turned it into an unduly strong one.

On the whole, the appearance of countervailing power as a political issue cannot be considered especially unhealthy al-though it will almost certainly be so regarded. At first glance there is something odious about the notion that the poor and the excluded improve their lot in a democracy only by winning power. But so far there has been much less reason to regret than to approve the results. The position of great groups in the community has been notably strengthened and improved. Those who lost power cannot be presumed to have enjoyed their loss. There was much outward evidence that they regretted it exceedingly. Some, however, may have lived to see that, set against the loss of their authority, is their greater prospect for an agreeable old age.

There remains, of course, the chance that power, developed and even encouraged to neutralize other power, will start on a career of its own. This is the spectre which has been raised by nearly every critic of the concept of countervailing power, even the friendliest ones. This danger may exist. No one can tell. It is some comfort that those who have worked most cohesively to develop countervailing power – the unions and the major farm organizations in particular – have so far comported themselves with some restraint. This is an area, we need remind ourselves, where anything that is novel has an unparalleled aspect of danger. Economic power even in its most elementary form evokes such fears. A leading American industrialist warned in 1903 that: 'Organized labour knows but one law and that is the law of physical force – the law of the Huns and the Vandals, the law of the savage. . . . Composed as it is of the men of muscle rather than the men of intelligence, and commanded by leaders who are at heart disciples of revolution, it is not strange that organized labour stands for principles that are in direct conflict with the natural laws of economics.'* Not even the professional alarmist would voice such views of the labour movement today. It is only in light of history that our fear of the countervailing power of weaker groups dissolves, that their effort to

* David M. Parry, President of the National Association of Manufacturers. Annual Address. *New York Times*, 15 April 1903.

establish their power in the market emerges as the stuff of which economic progress consists. It is by our experience, not our fears, that we should be guided.

# CHAPTER II

# The Case of Agriculture

I

THE effort of longest standing to develop countervailing power, not even excepting that of labour, has been made by the farmer. And his efforts have taken a striking diversity of forms. Because of its importance in itself, and because of the light it throws on the problem of building countervailing power, the case of agriculture is worth examining in more detail.

In both the markets in which he sells and those in which he buys, the individual farmer's market power in the typical case is intrinsically nil. In each case he is one among hundreds of thousands. As an individual he can withdraw from the market entirely, and there will be no effect on price – his action will, indeed, have no consequence for anyone but himself and his dependents.

Those from whom the farmer buys and those to whom he sells do, characteristically, have market power. The handful of manufacturers of farm machinery, of accessible fertilizer manufacturers or mixers, of petroleum suppliers, of insurance companies all exercise measurable control over the prices at which they sell. The farmer's market for his products – the meat-packing industry, the tobacco companies, the canneries, the fluid-milk distributors – is typically, although not universally, divided between a relatively small number of relatively large companies. There is no more vigorously debated question in economics than that of the jurisdiction which such companies exercise over their buying prices. That a measure of latent power exists for tacit or overt influence over such prices can hardly be denied. A canning factory must, after all, declare the price it will pay on a given day or during a given week or season for tomatoes. Implicit in such power of decision is some measure of influence over the price and the influence will be increased if the factory is the only one in the area or if it has a shrewd judgement as to the probable behaviour of other buyers. But even where the influence is difficult to see, it may be inherent in the greater ability of the buyer to decide to buy or not to buy. This, in turn, can have considerable effect on prices. The farmer has no equivalent discretion.

In our time, partly as a result of the new market power of the farmer and partly as a reaction to his very considerable political influence, the market power of those to whom he sells has come to be exercised with profound circumspection. This has not been true in the past. On the contrary, the farmer was often made to pay dearly for his lack of market power. It was this that led him to search long and hard for a formula for expressing effective countervailing power.

II

Indeed, the effort is nearly as old as settlement on this continent. Within a few years after the first colonists arrived in Virginia, the tobacco planters were petitioning the Crown for redress against the oppression of the 'unconscionable and cruel merchants' who bought their tobacco and supplied them with goods from England.* In 1631 the colonial authorities stipulated that no tobacco might be offered for purchase of English goods at a valuation of less than sixpence a pound. The tobacco growers, for the first but not the last time, were

* L. C. Gray, *Agriculture in the Southern United States to 1860* (Washington: Carnegie Institution, 1933), vol. I, p. 430.

seeking the support of public authority in an effort to bolster their bargaining position against their more powerful customers and suppliers. The result was the first but not the last support price for farm products in North America. The circumstances which motivated it were not different from those that led to the New Deal farm programme almost exactly three centuries later. In both cases the tobacco producers were seeking to redress the organic inequalities of bargaining power in a market where the many face the few.

It might be added that this first support price had other consequences which later experience has made familiar. The colonial authorities were speedily forced on from price to production control. In 1639, a primitive Agricultural Adjustment Act established a maximum production for that and the two following years of 1,200,000 pounds. Viewers were appointed to secure compliance on the individual plantations and given plenary authority to burn inferior grades of tobacco and up to one-half of any planter's crop.* Regimentation of the farmer is no latter-day development.

As the analysis of the last two chapters suggests, there are, in principle, three things which the farmer can do to offset his weakness in bargaining power. He can seek to build countervailing power in the market – in the tradition of the Virginia tobacco planters. Or he can seek to dissolve the original power of those to whom he sells or from whom he buys. Finally, he can attempt to get the advantages of the enhanced market power that are associated with changes in demand. To the extent that demand in the economy as a whole can be maintained at strong or inflationary levels, his position as a seller will be strong. This results from the shift of power from buyer to seller under conditions of inflation which, in relation to its effect on countervailing power, was examined in Chapter 9. Like other producers, the farmer

* ibid., p. 261.

is more disposed to emphasize his role as a seller than as a buyer and there are very good reasons why he should do so.

American farmers have tried all three methods of buttressing their market power. Under agrarian pressure the northern colonies, especially before the middle of the eighteenth century, were inveterately inflationist. The colonies of the Middle Atlantic were considerably less given to inflation but only, apparently, because stronger governors prevented the issue of paper money. The southern colonies, with some exceptions such as South Carolina, had comparatively stable currencies.* In these latter colonies, which depended heavily on their export trade in staples, there was no appreciable advantage to the farmers in inflation. The English sterling prices of tobacco and goods were what counted; these were beyond the reach of colonial monetary policy.

During much of the nineteenth century – successfully when Jackson was his candidate,† unsuccessfully when it was William Jennings Bryan – the farmer concentrated his efforts on expanding demand. Through the free banking of the Jacksonian era and the free coinage of Bryan, as well as in such shorter-lived episodes as the Greenback Movement in the seventies, he sought to increase the means of payment and therewith to alter the balance of bargaining power in his favour. Historians have all but invariably related this inflationary bias of the nineteenth-century agrarian to his desire to ease the burden of his indebtedness. This explanation, in its

* Cf. Richard A. Lester, *Monetary Experiments* (Princeton: Princeton University Press, 1939), p. 24.

† My colleague, Professor Arthur M. Schlesinger, Jr, has warned me against implying that Jackson himself was an inflationist. His supporters were; so were the effects of his successful attack on the Second Bank of the United States. However, Jackson himself was a conservative in monetary matters and indeed the exponent of a hard-money policy. His opposition to the Bank and to Nicholas Biddle arose not from the restraint they exercised on the inflationary note issues of the state banks but from the conviction that they had too much power.

neglect of the issue of relative bargaining power, is almost certainly incomplete.

In this century the farmer has largely lost interest in inflation. One reason is that inflation has ceased to be technically practicable by the old methods. With modern banking institutions and modern attitudes of borrowers and lenders, borrowing does not follow automatically when credit is available as it very nearly did in the time of Jackson. The volume of bank borrowing and the resulting movements in money supply have now become consequences, not causes, of other changes. As a result, the possibility of deliberately engineering an old-fashioned credit or currency inflation has largely disappeared. Inflation can still be brought about through the agency of large budget deficits, but these do not have the aura of easy costlessness of unlimited emissions of banknotes or unlimited coinage of silver. The frustrations of the Bryan campaigns, and the growing suspicion of the green magic of the money doctors, gradually weaned farmers away from their old faith in monetary experiment. As this happened, they turned to more forthright methods of equalizing their bargaining power.

Initially, this took the form of efforts to break down the market position of those with whom the farmer did business. In the latter part of the nineteenth century, and in the early decades of the present century, by far the strongest pressure for the regulation or dissolution of big business came from the farmbelt. The first and most spectacular manifestation of this was the Granger Movement. With almost revolutionary venom, the farmers of the early seventies turned on the railroads, commission merchants, warehousemen, farm machinery companies, and merchants with whom they did business. In seeking regulation of these enterprises the Grangers saw, quite clearly, that they possessed market power which the farmer did not have. To quote the historian of the movement, 'Just as the price which the farmer received for the commodities he sold seemed to him to be fixed by those to whom he sold, so also, he felt that the price of his supplies was fixed by those from whom he bought.'*

The Granger eruption was short-lived. It flared across Illinois, Iowa, Wisconsin, and the Eastern Great Plains, capturing state legislatures and passing laws to bring railroads, warehouses, and other enterprises under state control. But it soon succumbed to individualism and inexperience and to corrupt leadership. It was, however, the precursor of a considerably more durable effort to dissolve opposing market power. Farmers, far more than labour, the urban middle class, or any other group including the liberal intellectuals of the day, forced the passage of the Sherman Anti-Trust Act of 1890. It is perhaps not entirely an accident that meat packers, tobacco companies, the farm-machinery industry, milk distributors, and, in the early days, the railroads, all of whom buy from, sell to, or serve the farmer, have been prominent targets of this legislation. During its sixty-year history, the strongest regional support for the Sherman Act and its supplementing legislation has come from the farm states. However, this legislation can no longer be considered central in the farmer's strategy for equalizing market power. The Sherman Act and subsequent antitrust legislation still enjoy the support of farm organizations and, generally, of Western congressmen. But it reflects a passive and even somewhat nostalgic interest. Farmers have turned from the reduction of opposing market power to the building of their own.

III

In seeking to develop countervailing power it was natural

* Solon J. Buck, *The Granger Movement* (Cambridge: Harvard University Press, 1913), p. 18.

that farmers would at some stage seek to imitate the market organization and strategy of those with whom they did business. For purchase or sale as individuals, they would seek to substitute purchase and sale as a group. Livestock or milk producers would combine in the sale of their livestock or milk. The market power of large meat packers and milk distributors would be matched by the market power of a large selling organization of livestock producers and dairymen. Similarly, if purchases of fertilizers, feed, and oil were pooled, the prices of these products, hitherto named by the seller to the individual farmer, would become subject to negotiation.

The necessary instrument of organization was also available to the farmer in the form of the cooperative. The membership of the cooperative could include any number of farmers and it could be democratically controlled. All in all, the cooperative seemed an ideal device for exercising countervailing power. For a period in the twenties and early thirties there was a widespread belief among American farmers that marketing cooperatives were indeed the answer to their needs. Following the depression of 1921, a remarkable propagandist from California, Aaron Sapiro, pictured for the cooperative member precisely the kind of bargaining position enjoyed by the processor or manufacturer. '... We have stopped dumping in the State of California and have substituted the merchandising of agricultural products. That means centralized control of these crops so that they move to such markets of the world, and at such times, as the markets can absorb the crops at fair prices.'* Sapiro-type cooperatives, as they came to be called, were formed to market potatoes, tobacco, wheat, fruit, and other products. Few survived, as bargaining instruments, for more than a year or two.

* Ontario Department of Agriculture, *Addresses on Cooperative Marketing by Mr Aaron Sapiro* (Toronto, 1922).

As a device for getting economies of larger-scale operations in the handling of farm products or for providing and capitalizing such facilities as elevators, grain terminals, warehouses, and creameries, cooperatives have enjoyed a considerable measure of success. For exercising market power they have fatal structural weaknesses. The cooperative is a loose association of individuals. It rarely includes all producers of a product. It cannot control the production of its members and, in practice, it has less than absolute control over their decision to sell. All these powers over its own production are possessed, as a matter of course, by the corporation. A strong bargaining position requires ability to wait – to hold some or all of the product. The cooperative cannot make the non-members wait; they are at liberty to sell when they please and, unlike the members, they have the advantage of selling all they please. In practice, the cooperative cannot fully control even its own members. They are under the constant temptation to break away and sell their full production. This they do, in effect, at the expense of those who stand by the cooperative. These weaknesses destroyed the Sapiro cooperatives.

The farmer's purchasing cooperative is free from the organic weaknesses of the marketing or bargaining cooperative. In the marketing cooperative the non cooperator, or recusant, gets a premium for his non-conformance. In the buying cooperative he can be denied the patronage dividends which reflect the economies of effective buying and bargaining. In the purchase of feed, chemicals for fertilizers, petroleum products, and other farm supplies and insurance these cooperatives have enjoyed major success. As earlier noted, they have come to rank with the mass retailers as instruments for the effective expression of countervailing power. However, they redress the weakness of his position only as a buyer and only for part of his purchases. Their success in no wise compensated for the failure of the marketing co-operative as a bargaining instrument.

The failure of the voluntary cooperative as a device for expressing market power is important for, out of it, by remarkably direct steps, grew the agricultural programmes of the thirties. After the farmer had failed to organize market power by himself, it was wholly in the tradition of the development of countervailing power that he should turn to the government for assistance. And it was equally natural that the government should first think of helping the farmer to establish the kind of cooperatives which, by his unaided efforts, he had been unable to build. This was done in the Agricultural Marketing Act of 1929. The Federal Farm Board established under this legislation undertook to sponsor and capitalize a system of national cooperatives. The bargaining powers of the latter were, in turn, to be supplemented by government Stabilization Corporations.

Had this effort been successful, wheat, cotton, tobacco and other farm producers would have been represented in their markets by one or a few powerful sellers. Their power in such markets would not have been different in kind from that already enjoyed by the steel companies, the automobile companies, or the Aluminum Company of America in theirs. It would have been the obvious counterpart of the market power implicit in the position of those to whom the farmer sells. Even the most intellectually reluctant might then have agreed that the one position of power was in response to the other. It is appropriate that this legislation was enacted by a Republican Administration in which American business attitudes were dominant. Faced with the need for doing something for the farmer, the obvious course to Mr Hoover and his colleagues was to remake the farmer as nearly as possible in the image of the typical industrial corporation.

The cooperatives hastily synthesized by the Federal Farm Board were subject to the same weaknesses – they placed the same premium on non-conformance and had the same inability to control the output of either member or non-member – as the voluntary cooperatives. Both they and the Stabilization Corporations were also engulfed by the price collapse of 1930 and 1931. In 1933 the victorious Democrats put the power resources of the government fully at the disposal of agriculture. In one sense this was but a small additional step. The Agricultural Adjustment Act of 1933, and the subsequent agricultural legislation, merely eliminated the technical weakness which had led to the failure of the earlier voluntary or government-aided efforts. The now half-forgotten processing tax of the original legislation was levied against the production of all growers of basic crops.* The proceeds were distributed to those who submitted to control of production. By penalizing the non cooperator and so controlling production of all, the weaknesses of voluntary bargaining through the cooperative were eliminated. After the abandonment of the processing tax in 1936 (when it was declared unconstitutional), direct subsidies from the Treasury, paid only to cooperators, were used as a passive penalty on the non-participant. In more recent times government purchases or loans have provided price guarantees which, if supplies are large, are contingent on the willingness of producers to accept marketing quotas on what they sell. This again is a change of form, not of content; by offering itself as an alternative customer, the government is still engaged in the essential task of reinforcing the bargaining position of the farmer.

* So called. Initially wheat, cotton, corn, hogs, rice, tobacco, and milk and milk products were so designated although all were not subject to the tax. See Edwin G. Nourse, Joseph S. Davis, and John D. Black, *Three Years of Agricultural Adjustment Administration* (Washington: The Brookings Institution, 1937), p. 42.

IV

Such, in brief, is the extraordinarily consistent record of the farmer's efforts to develop countervailing power. Curiously enough, the whole effort is still viewed, even to some extent by farmers themselves, as vaguely artificial. While the word 'emergency' has now disappeared from agricultural legislation, there is still a subjective feeling that some day it will pass away. The fact that the modern legislation is now of many years standing, that behind it is a long history of equivalent aspiration, that there is not a developed country. in the world where its counterpart does not exist, that no political party would think of formally attacking it, are all worth pondering by those who regard such legislation as abnormal.

So far from being abnormal, given the market power of the industries among which the American farmer is cited and the probability of fluctuating demand, it is organic.* There

---

* This reference to fluctuations in demand seems worth a special word of emphasis. The contention that the farmer's market position and hence his market power is broadly different from that of his suppliers and customers has been denied or put down as unproven by a number of critics, not all of them men who have conditioned themselves to hear nothing that is evil or inconvenient about the price system. This follows partly from a tendency to see market power only when it is obtrusively exercised and to assume that what is invisible is inevitably benign. It is partly the result of a failure to reflect fully on the evidence. None of these critics would deny that when aggregate demand in the economy falls, the terms of trade turn against the farmer and that his prices also fall much more sharply than do the prices he pays or the margins of those who handle or process his products. Those patterns of economic behaviour are as nearly taken for granted as anything in economics. Yet they can be only explained by a broad difference in market structure which gives the farmer's suppliers and customers the power to control the adjustment of their prices to the fall in demand. This power, of course, the farmer does not have.

would be many advantages in recognizing this. If we fail to regard government support to the bargaining power of the farmer and other groups as normal, we shall almost certainly neglect to search for the principles that should govern the subsidy of private groups by public power. We shall also be less likely to correct the considerable number of abuses and faults which have been associated with government aid to countervailing power – abuses and faults which have been especially numerous and serious in agricultural legislation. Many who might have concerned themselves with these faults have continued to suppose that the remedy is to abolish the entire activity. Like the executioners during the French Revolution, they have offered the guillotine as a cure for headache. This is not the best frame of mind in which to seek improvement in what is certain to continue.

# CHAPTER 12

# The Role of Decentralized Decision

## I

THE time has now come to apply the argument of the last several chapters to what has been the most heated subject of domestic controversy in the United States in recent decades, namely the role of the state in relation to private economic decision. In the past, private business management has had decisive responsibilities in the economy. It has decided what to produce, in what quantity, at what price, paying what wages, and with what investment to increase future production. In addition it has had the responsibility for organizing and managing production. Whether the decisions required in these tasks be difficult or simple, a great many decisions are required. The most distinctive characteristic of the businessman – the thing that most sharply distinguishes him from the lawyer, college professor, or, generally speaking, the civil servant – is his capacity for decision. The effective businessman is invariably able to make up his mind, often on limited evidence, without uncertainty as to his own wisdom. It is a part of this talent not to reflect on past mistakes or even to concede that a mistake has been made.

The presumption of a rule of competition in the economy led to the further presumption that these business decisions would be at least generally in the public interest. Poor decisions or mistakes harmed the businessman, not the public; good decisions benefited all. As a result, state interference with business decision was either redundant or positively harmful. With the increasing implausibility of the assumption of competition, the ancient basis for the businessman's claim to independence became subject to serious erosion. The question that now arises is to what extent independent business decision is rehabilitated when countervailing power, not competition, is recognized as a restraint on the private exercise of economic power. When this is answered there still remains the further question as to what interference with the businessman's autonomy is required, not to prevent the misuse of power, but to insure that the economy finds its peacetime norm without too much unemployment or too much inflation. This chapter takes up the role of the state in relation to private market power; the two final chapters of this essay examine its role in relation to general economic performance and stability.

## II

The phenomenon of countervailing power does provide a negative justification for leaving authority over production decisions in private hands. Like competition countervailing power operates to prevent the misuse of such power. The firm or group of firms that is using its market power to enhance prices or depress wages, as the last three chapters have shown, both force and reward the development of the strength that neutralizes such power. If this did not happen, private decisions could and presumably would lead to the unhampered exploitation of the public or of workers, farmers, and others who are intrinsically weak as individuals. Such decisions would be a proper object of state interference or would soon so become. This interference is now made unnecessary because those affected by the decisions are able, in effect, to look after themselves.

Since the development of countervailing power is irregular and incomplete, it does not provide a blanket case for the exclusion of state interference with private decision. Moreover the state must be expected to participate in the development of countervailing power. None the less, it is countervailing power which, in the typical modern industrial market, regulates the power of private decision. As such it provides the negative justification for leaving decision in private hands, for it prevents these decisions from working harm on others.

I venture to suggest that this rationale of private authority over production – or of private enterprise – will be almost equally unpalatable to liberals and conservatives. This is often the case with reality. Some liberals have already detected here a nefarious whitewash of crypto-monopoly and bigness. They are reminded, however, that they also have here the explanation of why, in a triumph of conscience and pragmatism over doctrine, they themselves have so often turned up, so inconsistently, on the side of trade unions, farm legislation, and other efforts to build seeming monopoly power.

To conservatives this argument should be attractive. In resting their case for private authority over production decisions on competition, they have had all the tactical mobility of a rider whose horse has been shot out from under him. The statistics of market concentration are notably unfavourable to their case. There is the opposing weight of modern market theory. This receives verification from the observably tenuous, nonexistent, or distorted character of competition in many markets – plus the highly visible preference of businessmen, as Walter Lippmann once noted, for as little of it as possible. Socialists have not been slow to find and exploit the tactical weaknesses of the conservative case. In the Marxian lexicon, capitalism and competition are mutually exclusive concepts; the Marxian attack has not been on capitalism but on monopoly capitalism. The fact that the power of the genus of monopoly is ubiquitous has not been difficult to show. So long as competition remains the conservative's defence, the left is bound to have a near monopoly of the evidence and the logic.

However, I cannot think that conservatives will find a defence of private decision that rests on countervailing power wholly pleasant. It makes indispensable the market power of unions, farmers, mass buyers, and others. Like competition this power is uncomfortable whenever it is effective. The present analysis also legitimatizes government support to countervailing power. This is certain to be regarded for some time to come as an undesirable extension of state activity even though it is already a commonplace one. I hazard the guess that the leader of the average large corporation will, for a time, prefer the implausible defence that he is a competitor in the classical sense, a mere barometer of market pressures, to the plausible one that his power, though considerable, is deployed against others who are strong enough to resist any harmful exercise of such power. There is nothing an economist should fear so much as applause, and I believe I am reasonably secure.

### III

The foregoing deals only with the negative case for private authority over production decisions. It is negative, for it shows only the resistance to a damaging exercise of private market power where there is a full development of countervailing power. In the competitive model there was a strong affirmative case for private production decision. Competition produced the most efficient use of resources; any interference by the state with private decisions concerning production could not therefore be beneficial and must accordingly be harmful.* In the early part of this century classical and

---

* There were always some theoretical exceptions, among them instances of long-run decreasing costs and of wide divergencies between private and social costs of production.

socialist economists wrangled at length over the question of whether a planned economy could devise any method of distributing resources and for accounting for costs of production that would be an effective substitute for what occurred under the price system. Even socialists were inclined to concede that the case for socialism stood or fell on their ability to do so.

No case for an *ideal* distribution and employment of resources – for maximized social efficiency – can be made when countervailing power rather than competition is accepted as the basic regulator of the economy. Countervailing power does operate in the right direction. When a powerful retail buyer forces down the prices of an industry which had previously been enjoying monopoly returns, the result is larger sales of the product, a larger and broadly speaking a more desirable use of labour, materials, and plant in production. But no one can suppose that this happens with precision. Thus a theoretical case exists for government intervention in private decision. It becomes strong where it can be shown that countervailing power is not fully operative.

In our time there has been a considerable and very possibly a growing tendency to criticize private business decision. In recent years there has been recurrent dissatisfaction with decisions of the steel industry on prices and on provision of new capacity, with the uneven performance of the construction industry, the railroads, even with the price and design of automobiles. There is no *a priori* reason to suppose that this criticism is ill-founded. It cannot be argued that the undisturbed private judgement in these cases is necessarily the best one; the social judgement, reflected in the attitudes of government, may well be theoretically better.

It has been shown, however, that technical development may compensate, or more than compensate, for more evident shortcomings of private decision and that wealth provides us with some latitude in these matters. Much more important, there is a strong administrative case for private decision.

Although little cited, even by conservatives, administrative considerations now provide capitalism with by far its strongest defence against detailed interference with private business decision. To put the matter bluntly, in a parliamentary democracy with a high standard of living there is no administratively acceptable alternative to the decision-making mechanism of capitalism. No method of comparable effectiveness is available to decentralize authority over final decisions.

Even where the concentration of control over industry is relatively great, the final authority over production decisions is held at a comparatively large number of points. This is of great significance. The decisions of the General Motors Corporation on the power, design, price, model changes, production schedules, and the myriad of other details concerning its automobiles are final. There is no appeal; the career or reputation of no higher authority is at stake. Were there such recourse, the process of reaching final decisions in a modern economy with a wide variety of products would be almost incredibly difficult. To deny the right of resort to ultimate authority would be to deny, from within the fabric of government, an accepted democratic right, that of free petition.

The process of decision-making has two dimensions, timing and quality. For relatively simple and undifferentiated types of production – the production of electric power, for example – the quality of the decision is normally more important than its timeliness. There the administrative problems of public management can be solved. Quite the reverse is true of consumers' goods. A poor decision is normally to be preferred to a late one. Any considerable centralization of authority over the decisions that are required in the production of the great variety of American consumer products – over what to produce, of what design, when, where, and with what investment for each – is something that it would seem hard for even an ardent socialist to contemplate. It can be argued that decentralization of decision might be possible, and might eventually be accepted even by a people and a legislature accustomed to the full rights of appeal, for all except key decisions. Only questions of wages, prices, and the broad contours of production and investment would be subject to central design. This is possible and for certain larger objectives of economic stabilization a broadly parallel pattern of action may be necessary. But such a proposal really misses the point. The objective of social control over production decisions is to make the resulting decisions more responsive to social needs and desires. If for administrative reasons government, having centralized decision, must then put the decision-making outside the reach of public opinion and pressures, it has abandoned the very job which it set out to perform.

Because the debate over socialism and planning has turned so heavily on such economic considerations as incentives and possibilities of accounting and pricing, these administrative considerations have been largely overlooked. Yet, as noted, there is every indication that in our time they are decisive. If, as here argued, any substantial degree of central authority over production decisions is administratively impossible in a community with a high, variegated, and variform standard of living, then the corollary is that such planning may be entirely feasible in a community with a fairly primitive standard of living. Centralized decision would become administratively possible where production is confined to a relatively small number of relatively standard products. Checking once more with experience, one finds it is communities with a low and simple standard of living – Russia, Eastern Europe, and now

China – that have turned (or been turned) to socialism. The advanced industrial countries, by contrast, have not done so even where they have an ideological commitment to socialism. There is a popular cliché, deeply beloved by conservatives, that socialism and communism are the cause of a low standard of living. It is much more nearly accurate to say that a low and simple standard of living makes socialism and communism feasible.

The decisive role of administration in countries with high living standards is admirably illustrated by the Scandinavian countries, and by the glacial gradualism with which socialist governments in these lands have proceeded towards public ownership. The recent history of the United Kingdom is even more instructive. The depth of the commitment of British workers to some form of central planning is not open to question nor is the sincerity of their leaders. In no other country, perhaps not even in Russia, was capitalism more thoroughly defeated as an idea among a voting majority of the people than in Britain after the thirties. But both the pace and form of British socialism when it came to power were sharply circumscribed by the problems of administering it. After the Labour victory in 1945, it soon became evident that the rate at which industries would be taken into public ownership would be determined primarily by administrative considerations. A growing appreciation of the scale and complexity of the administrative apparatus required not only slowed the pace of nationalization but also, it would appear, tempered the enthusiasm of British socialists for the policy itself.

The effect of administrative considerations on the selection of industries to be nationalized has been even more interesting. The first block of industries marked for nationalization – coal-mining, transport, electricity, gas utilities, overseas communications, and the Bank of England – were, with the exception of the first, ones in which public ownership involved a minimum of administrative difficulty or even of change. Public ownership of these industries is commonplace in advanced industrial countries. These industries were familiar socialist targets; it would be unfair to suggest that they were consciously selected because they would be easy to manage. But the fact that they presented no insurmountable administrative problems was almost certainly a passive factor in their selection. Industries that have since been suggested for nationalization – sugar and cement, for example – have been ones in which the administrative problem would have been comparatively simple. This, it would seem most probable, was a central if still somewhat subjective consideration.

On the other hand, the Labour Government left the consumer industries – automobiles, radios, clothing, textiles, and the like – severely alone. Here any centralization of authority over production decisions – decisions that would reflect, in their number, the variety of products and the need for accommodating production, design, and style to the shifting tastes of consumers at home and abroad – would be most difficult. It can be assumed that few British leaders, whatever their political convictions, wished to shoulder such responsibilities. Thus, though no British Labour Member and not all Conservatives profess any affection for capitalism, there are not many who would advance, with much confidence, any administratively feasible alternative.

The same administrative considerations, in the last analysis, protect the American businessman in his present authority. The exercise of that authority is made tolerable by the restraints imposed by countervailing power and by competition. Social inefficiency, which is great in the static view, is offset by a high rate of technical advance. Those are imperfect arrangements; schematically better ones could be imagined and have been. But there remains the problem of administration – how theoretically more satisfactory systems could, in fact, be organized and run. The modern case for capitalism is not, as so many would like to believe, based on the astonishing perfection of its design. Nor is it based on divine ordinance. Nor does it survive because those who would overthrow the system have been effectively routed out and exposed. It survives because there isn't anything administratively workable to take its place.

Because the issue is a pragmatic one, the exclusion of full state control over private decision does not exclude all control. This is not a matter of principle but of results. Each case can and should be settled on its own merits. In industries, electric-power utilities for example, where market power is inherent in the structure of the industry and where the development of countervailing power cannot be counted on by the great mass of consumers,* government control of private decisions must be expected. The fact that decision-making in such industries has been·shown to be well within the competence of public authority makes possible the further step towards public ownership, a step that has become commonplace in the United States. In other industries – low-cost housing for example – government management can be readily justified even though the decisions involved may be numerous and difficult. Here effective countervailing power has not developed and the product in question is of peculiar importance. The administrative problems created by centralization do not put the advocate of government intervention or of public ownership out of business. They do, in combination with the theory of countervailing power, direct and in

* It is noteworthy that large users, by the development of standby plant, by the threat to move, or by other assertions of their indispensability as a buyer are frequently able to develop effective countervailing power even in this field.

a measure confine his energies to those industries and areas where there is a genuine need for his remedy.

IV

Clearly, even the great administrative problems of public ownership might have to be tackled and surmounted were the alternative continuing malperformance like that of the thirties or the inflation that was experienced following the Second World War. The resolution of the problem of market power does not resolve these questions. We have, within the economy, no mechanism which acts autonomously to insure proper performance; it is evident from experience as well as from theory that the peacetime norm of the American economy is not necessarily stability at a high level of production and employment. This latter, clearly, is taken as a desideratum by a great majority of Americans. The last task of this book is to see what assertion of state power, and what interference with private authority, is necessary to have high and reasonably stable production and employment at reasonably stable prices.

# CHAPTER 13

## The Role of Centralized Decision

I

THE American tradition in economics involves a remarkable balance of candour and conservatism. It is sufficiently candid to keep the American businessman constantly alarmed about the ideas of economists but sufficiently conservative to make the alarm unwarranted. In this tradition, American economists have expressed deep and continuing alarm over the problem of private market power. But they have rarely looked with favour on comprehensive government interference with private business decisions.

On the contrary, they have engaged in an avid search for a formula for correcting the shortcomings in the behaviour of the economy while leaving private authority over production decisions unimpaired. There has been, in modern times, something close to an agreed design for achieving this aim. Economists have hoped, many against hope, that competition, backed as necessary by rigorous enforcement of the antitrust laws, would serve to maximize social efficiency and prevent the abuse of private power in the market. Our conclusions on these matters are now complete. Meanwhile inflation and depression, the larger failures in performance, would be taken care of by the further formula identified with the name of Keynes. To this I now turn.

The eagerness with which Keynes's doctrines were discussed by American economists, following the publication of his last great book in 1936,* is to be explained as much by the

* *The General Theory of Employment, Interest, and Money* (New York: Harcourt, Brace and Co., 1936).

urgency of the dilemma from which he provided a seeming escape as by the plausibility of the solution itself. For there was a very great difference between the urgency of the questions of social efficiency and market power associated with the abandonment of the competitive model and those presented by the depression. The first were important principally in the realm of ideas. Competition seemed not to be effective but the consequences, for reasons that will now be clear, seemed not to be disastrous. But the depression really existed; to find a remedy for it was a categorical imperative.

The essence of the Keynesian formula consists in leaving private decisions over production, including those involving prices and wages, to the men who now make them. The businessman's apparent area of discretion is in nowise narrowed. Centralized decision is brought to bear only on the climate in which those decisions are made; it insures only that the factors influencing free and intelligent decision will lead to a private action that contributes to economic stability. Thus, in times of depression, increased government expenditures or decreased taxation will cause or allow an increase in demand. The resulting business decisions on production and investment, though quite uncontrolled, will result in increased production and employment.

In time of full or overfull employment and rising prices the course of uncontrolled decisions, which otherwise would be in the direction of increasing prices and wages, will be reshaped by higher taxes and lower government expenditures. These latter will make sales difficult. Price increases will be unwise; so will decisions to expand investment and employment. In this way the government, by influencing the total demand for goods, gets the pattern of decision which it seeks without at any stage intervening in the decision itself.

There are many questions of method raised by such a policy and for many years now economists have been debating them vigorously. What are the relative advantages of increasing government expenditures or reducing taxes for getting an increase in demand? To what extent can the increase in expenditure or the reduction in taxes be made automatic? (Unemployment compensation payments, for example, are automatic for they increase automatically with a decline in employment.) Is it possible to anticipate inflation or deflation or must action be taken after the fact? How much unemployment or inflation can be tolerated? All this accepts the policy and concerns itself only with application. The chief doubt about the policy itself which the generality of economists have permitted themselves in recent years is whether the government can have, not the intelligence, but the will to carry through the policy. To increase taxes and cut government expenditures to halt inflation has been supposed, in particular, to be peculiarly challenging to a politician.

If the Keynesian formula is workable, then the last of the major reasons for alarm over American capitalism would seem to dissolve. The economy, in peacetime, can be kept somewhere close to an equilibrium of capacity production or (the more common synonym) to full employment. There will still be some reluctance to concede this large responsibility to government. For some, Keynes will doubtless remain a sinister figure, more dangerous even than our classical symbols of dangerous thoughts, Darwin, Bryan, and Marx. But not everyone can be happy. And even among businessmen there is, as noted earlier, a wide acceptance of Keynes. The Committee for Economic Development, the newest and in respect of ideas the most influential of national business organizations, from the beginning has had a deep though unproclaimed commitment to Keynes.* The basic tenets of Keynesian policy have been embraced, though again without invoking the name of Keynes, by a Republican Administration. Were acceptance of Keynes completely unanimous it would be unfortunate for his followers. They have long been able to wear a mantle of radicalism that has been unique in all history in its comfort. Their prophet, a self-made millionaire, sought for nothing so earnestly as to save liberal capitalism. His followers were equally persuaded of their mission. They could thus claim that they were being attacked for their efforts to preserve the *status quo;* they were martyrs to their own enlightened conservatism.

## II

There is reason to think that Keynes did, indeed, provide a plausible solution to the problem of deflation and depression. It is a solution which, let it be emphasized, could tax our reserves of vigour, imagination, and courage. But it is a solution. However, the application of Keynes's formula to the economy is not symmetrical. It does not deal equally well with the problem of inflation. Nor does it comprehend the dangers of the boom in the modern economy.

Those shortcomings have not yet been fully recognized. Professional economists, like businessmen, farmers, and workers have, as noted, been subject to the depression psychosis.

* Cf. *Jobs and Markets*. By the C.E.D. Research Staff. (New York: McGraw-Hill Book Co., Inc., 1946.) Although a staff study, this book reflected fairly the early trend of C.E.D. thinking on economic stabilization. Even an N.A.M. study of the same period, while disapproving of the use of government expenditures for stabilization, does endorse the Keynesian equivalent of variable tax rates. Rates would be increased in good times, reduced during depression. *The American Individual Enterprise System*. Economic Principles Commission. New York: McGraw-Hill Book Co., Inc., 1946, p. 982.

As a result, discussion of what has come to be called Keynesian policy has been, in practice, mostly a discussion of policies to counter depression. The problem of controlling inflation has been dismissed, far more frequently than has yet been realized, by the assumption that it requires measures that are the equal and opposite of the depression remedies. On close examination, and particularly when the role of countervailing power in the economy is recognized, this turns out to be not the case. As the depression psychosis is eroded by the passage of time, the old-fashioned speculative boom has re-emerged as a threat to economic stability. This danger too has gone largely unrecognized. However, it will be convenient, first, to examine the application of the Keynesian formula to depression.

A great many things have happened to the economy of the United States since the years of the Great Depression and to a quite remarkable extent they have been favourable to the employment of the Keynesian formula as a counter to depression. There is first the knowledge that a formula exists – the conviction that the government can, will, and should act to prevent a slump. This in turn has a bearing on investment and even possibly on consumer behaviour. In particular, if there is confidence that the government will defend the level of demand there is an appreciably smaller chance of hasty inventory liquidation or investment curtailment in response to some unfavourable news or development.

Next, there is the great increase in the scale of government expenditures. These have come to exceed, in dollar amount, the total of all spending, public and private, at the depths of the Great Depression. In the short run these outlays are wholly reliable. Private investment, by contrast, can be subject to comparatively sudden revision. The result can be general contraction, even collapse, of demand. Like rafters under the roof, public spending has a marked stiffening effect on the structure of the economy. It is also evident that this is a field of affairs where virtue, for the conservative at least, wears an extraordinarily unattractive garb. This is especially the case with the next buttress of the Keynesian formula, which is the vastly greater reliance than hitherto on corporate and personal income taxes.

The yield of both these taxes at given rates increases or decreases more than proportionately with an increase or decrease in business activity. The personal income tax, since it reflects the movement of people up to higher or down to lower tax brackets, has a very strong tendency to increase or reduce itself at precisely the time when such changes are in order. In so doing it cuts more deeply into private demand the more excessive the demand, and frees income for private use in larger amounts the larger the drop in demand. It is doubtful, incidentally, if any single device has done so much to secure the future of capitalism as this tax. It is regarded, in our time, as the great leveller of incomes. But the income tax is also – a much neglected point – the great buttress of income inequality. The rich man no longer has the embarrassing task of justifying his higher income on grounds of superior morals, ability, diligence, or higher natural right. He need only point to the tax he has to pay. And the man of modest income now reflects that his relative poverty saves him a terrifying tax bill. As an added dividend, the tax works silently and automatically on the side of economic stability. Conservatives should build a statue to it and to its inspired progenitor, President William Howard Taft.

There have been other reinforcements. In the years prior to the Great Depression the economic system of the United States had a variety of disastrous weaknesses. The corporate structure was fragile. So was the banking system. The balance of payments was heavily dependent on highly dubious foreign loans. The financing of new investment was intricately associated with arrangements for victimizing the investor.*

During the thirties legislation, abetted by bitter recollection, corrected the more glaring of these weaknesses. And further important steps towards stabilization came as a consequence of, or as a reaction to, the miseries of these years. Thus unemployment insurance secured the worker a minimum of income while out of work. The knowledge that he has this safeguard now enables him to spend his current income with greater assurance. Given a reduction in employment there is a floor, albeit still a rather low one, under a large part of consumer expenditure. Support prices for farm products assure most commercial farmers of substantial prices and incomes should demand for their products fall. In the event of a serious depression government spending for the support of farm prices would rise both automatically and quite astronomically. By comparison with the thirties at least, farmers' expenditures would remain relatively stable. In the fifteen years following the advent of the New Deal a very considerable amount of stability was built into the aggregate of expenditures in the American economy.

### III

Thus, in the years since the Second World War, the context for using the Keynesian formula has been far more favourable than in the early thirties when the New Deal made its first halting efforts. Some of the credit, it will be pointed out, must go to the large military expenditures with their equivocal relationship to continued existence. In the absence of this spending there might have been a slump. The magnitudes of other

* I venture to refer the reader to my book *The Great Crash, 1929* (Houghton Mifflin, 1955; Penguin Books, 1961), in which I have dealt with these weaknesses in more detail.

fiscal action – of public spending in particular – to overcome such a slump might have been impossibly large.

However, had the world been at peace, funds going for
arms *could* have gone in considerable quantities for highways,
housing, the inevitable ditches and dams of the Corps of
Engineers and the Reclamation Service, for assistance to
poor and undeveloped lands, and for many other useful
civilian purposes. More demand could have been sustained by
tax reductions which would allow (and be so designed as to
cause) consumers to spend what had previously been sur-
rendered to the state. The opportunity for such reductions,
in contrast with earlier periods in our history, is mercifully
large. Such a policy would have required imagination and
vigour. There are still self-confessed realists who would have
seen the end of military spending as a heaven-sent opportunity for a general repression of all public spending, an aggressive programme of debt reduction, a consequent reduction
in aggregate demand and, in sum, for the promotion of a general depression. These policies would somehow have had to
be quarantined. Yet none of this seems as romantic as once
it did.

The context, therefore, has been one in which the economy
could be propped with a fair chance of success. But it must
also be emphasized that in the years following the Second
World War, with the exception of the Korean interlude,
it was propping that was required. The problem was to
support and not restrain the level of aggregate demand. This
point has been effectively stressed by Professor Alvin H.
Hansen for the period immediately following the Second
World War:

'The remarkable thing about the period from the end of the
Second World War to the Korean crisis is . . . that, notwithstanding the large backlog of deferred demand for plant,
equipment, houses, and consumers' durables, and despite the

vast military and foreign aid programmes, the American economy, after a catching-up period of only a couple of years, proved fully equal to the task. This was a tremendous demonstration of how vast a volume of aggregate demand is necessary to keep the ... American economy fully employed.'*

A situation in which propping of demand rather than restraint is required is also far more fortunate than most people, including most economists, have ever suspected. Under such circumstances, the regulatory force of countervailing power remains at work. The needed action to expand demand is also in the main stream of American – indeed, of all – politics. The appropriate tax and expenditure policies have the approval of workers and farmers. As a matter of principle they are approved by a good many businessmen and as a matter of practice, where their own markets are involved, by a good many more. Neither an increase of expenditure nor a reduction in taxes places the average Congressman in political jeopardy. The bureaucracy faces both without dismay. Standing against such action in the past has been only a barrier of ideas – the idea that such action, and the unbalance of revenues and expenditures which resulted, violated the canons of fiscal sanity. Given Say's Law and a tendency for the economy to find its equilibrium at full employment, such action to support demand was not only unnecessary but positively harmful. Anyone who questions the power of ideas should consider how successfully, for how long and against what political odds, convictions based on Say's Law held the fort against the notion that budgets might wisely be unbalanced during depression. But Say has been dethroned.

Such was the context of economic policy in the years following the Second World War, years in which the achievements of the American economy were marked. There is no

* *Business Cycles and the National Income* (New York: W. W. Norton Co., 1951), pp. 507–8.

reason, however, to suppose that this comparatively favourable situation is either inevitable or immutable. On the contrary there is reason to believe that it is not. Over time a situation in which the economy is successfully propped may bring a liberalization of investment and consumer attitudes with the result that propping is no longer necessary. There is always the chance, in the world as it is, that expenditures occasioned by the *force majeure* of defence or small wars may raise demand beyond the current capacity of the economy. (I exclude the case of major war which, without doubt, would alter all of the parameters.) It is necessary, accordingly, to consider the problem of policy in a context where restraint, not support, is required.

# CHAPTER 14

# The Problem of Restraint

I

THERE are a number of forces which are capable of causing demand in the modern economy to rise to the point where it presses with greater or less severity on the current capacity of the economy. One obvious possibility is defence or war spending. Unlike other public outlays these, at least within limits, allow no choice. If the state is being forced to spend for military purposes it obviously cannot (or should not) reduce these expenditures for reasons of fiscal policy. And if military expenditures are a large fraction of all public expenditures, which will be the case under such circumstances, all hope of influencing the level of demand by regulating the level of public spending disappears.

In modern times nearly all of our experience with excess demand has been the result of military spending. However, there are two other possibilities of importance. One is a matter of experience. One could be.

In the autumn of 1950 there was an upsurge in demand which brought the sharpest price increases in modern American history. The federal budget was balanced at the time; the increase in military spending, as a result of the Korean War which had begun that summer, was still negligible. The cause was the sudden rush of consumers to buy goods and of businessmen to acquire inventories, both motivated by a fear of a recurrence of civilian shortages. The consumer buying was nourished by the roughly $150 billions in liquid assets – demand and saving deposits, shares in savings and loan companies, and government bonds – owned by individuals at the time. The liquid assets of American consumers remain high; consequently there is a continuing although not necessarily a strong possibility that some occurrence will induce efforts to convert assets into goods. The result could be a sudden and serious excess of demand.

The upsurge in the autumn of 1950 came about because of a radical change in expectations, from anticipation of peaceful plenty to wartime scarcity. There could be a similar though also somewhat more gradual result from a change in long-run expectations concerning prosperity and depression.

Thus consumers have long been encouraged to hold a relatively large volume of liquid assets as a precaution against the return of hard times. It has been an aspect of the depression psychosis. A release from this fear would for some bring a reduced effort to add to these holdings. For others it would bring a willingness to reduce liquid holdings and for yet others an enhanced willingness to take the counterpart step of incurring consumer debt. In an atmosphere of expanding confidence these steps could proceed rather rapidly – net savings could fall sharply. Such a development would inevitably be reinforced by parallel steps, occasioned by parallel attitudes, on the part of businessmen. Were American businessmen once completely persuaded of the prospect of permanent full employment, there would be a large and possibly a very large increase in inventory and long-term investment. Liquid business assets would be quickly committed; there would be vigorous borrowing for investment. The promise of permanent prosperity would be an assurance of good earnings. The stock market could be expected to respond. In the general nature of speculation, an initial increase so stimulated can be expected, under some circumstances at least, to develop a dynamic of its own. Speculators are attracted by the prospect for capital gains. The fact that the market is rising and capital gains are being made becomes the new reality. People seek to share in the capital gains and the market rises as the result of their efforts to participate. Gains from the appreciation in security values find their way into consumers' goods markets.

In other words, a general release from depression psychosis could be a cause of an inflationary increase in demand. By spilling over into speculation it could also be an original cause of serious trouble later on. The breaking of a speculative bubble is likely to bring a radical and highly inconvenient curtailment in investment demand. The demand for consumers' products, particularly by those whose speculative gains have become losses, also suffers. These are not remote contingencies. They could happen. They might even be inherent in a successful policy to prevent and to contain depression and the confidence that such a policy would engender. One test of the danger will be when men assert that it has ceased to exist and the more fatuous in high office suggest that those are communists who demur. As this is written, the signs, it so happens, are not entirely favourable.

In any case, one of the great sources of stability in the American economy in the years following the Second World War was the invaluable fear that the depression of the thirties might recur. For years we have talked of the virtues of confidence. In fact, we have been blessed by the fruits of caution. But this is a wasting resource. With time and prosperity the fear of a recurrence of depression is bound to fade. As noted, this signifies serious trouble.

We still live under the shadow of the boom with its possibility of an excess of demand in the short run and its built-in potential for collapse in the longer run. To this must be added the continuing danger that demand will become excessive under the pressure of war or preparation for war or because of some sudden retreat into goods by investors and consumers. The last task of this book is to examine the consequent problem of restraint.

## II

There is no way of knowing whether the contingency of an excess of demand is more or less probable than that of a shortage. This depends on events far beyond the field of economics. There is no doubt, however, that the problem of restraining demand when this is required is far more formidable than that of propping it. It also presents a much more pregnant threat to the system of decentralized decision. One of the risks which the economist runs, in citing problems of economic policy or performance, is to be held responsible for their solution. The first edition of this book was viewed sternly by several critics for citing the difficulties of contending with an excess of demand without offering any wholly satisfactory solution. The gamut must now be run again for it is the sad fact that within the broad framework of democratic and especially of American politics no very satisfactory solution does exist. Those that are most satisfactory, at least to their authors, are the least consistent with our political traditions.

When there is an excess of demand, as noted, the self-regulatory mechanism based on countervailing power ceases to be effective. It takes on, instead, a malignant form which becomes part of the dynamic of inflation itself. As demand for goods increases, and becomes increasingly inelastic, those who are exercising countervailing power on behalf of buyers are no longer able to make their power effective. The balance between those who are exercising it on behalf of sellers and their customers is upset. The consequences, especially in the labour market, are profound. Employers who are faced with demand for higher wages can pay them and pass the added cost along in prices with impunity. They do. The higher wages become, in turn, the source of the higher income which helps sustain demand at the new prices. What, under all conditions of deflationary pressure, is an admirable device for countering the power of buyers of labour becomes a device for accelerating and perpetuating inflation.

This interaction of wages upon prices and prices upon wages has, it must be emphasized, a dynamic of its own whenever production is at or near the current capacity of plant and the labour force. A comparison of the market regulated by countervailing power with the market of the competitive model will show the nature of this self-agitating movement. A net increase in total demand, in an economy regulated by competition, will in the short run bring a proportionate increase in prices. Prices will rise to the point where, when multiplied by the currently available production, the value of the available supply will equal total demand. There will be no further effects within the period in which total output cannot be appreciably increased. A further increase in prices will require a further net increase in demand. The whole process is smoothly reversible. A reduction in net demand equal to the preceding increase will bring a like reduction in prices. All this holds equally whether the starting point be, by some historical standard, from a position of high demand or low. Wages of workers will rise and fall, and purely as a consequence of the movements in prices. Being unorganized, the workers do not have power to interfere.

Where markets are regulated by countervailing power, by contrast, a net increase in demand at any time when the labour force and plant are being used to approximate capacity brings a further train of consequences. As noted, both labour and management are in a position to seek and obtain increases in prices or wages. It makes little difference which takes the initiative; one forces the other to follow. An initial wage increase for labour means higher costs for management. These provide a need, or a justification, for price advances. An initial price advance by management means higher profits and, prospectively at least, higher living costs for labour. These provide both an incentive and a justification for wage demands.

In the nature of man, if for no other reason, both labour and management will normally seek something more than mere compensation for the last change to their disadvantage. Thus, as has been well demonstrated by modern experience, management after paying a wage increase ordinarily recoups something more than the resulting cost increase in prices. The result is an increase in profits which, along with the further increase in living costs, remains as a kind of residual incentive to labour to start the next round.

There is no definite limitation on the magnitude of the price and wage increases in any of these rounds. This depends, quite indeterminately, on the accident of the bargain that is struck – more accurately the coalition that is reached – between management and labour.

With the competitive model, as noted, the increase in price associated with a given net addition in demand is proportional. With countervailing power and the economy working at the capacity of plant and labour force, the increase in prices may, depending on the accident of the bargain, be less, just, or more than proportional. With the competitive model the increase in prices follows the increase in demand and that is the end of it. With countervailing power the initial impulse sets in motion a further train of impulses going further in the same direction. With the competitive model, the process was smoothly reversible; a decrease in demand brought a proportionate decrease in prices. With countervailing power, demand may decrease but, if there is still pressure on capacity, prices will continue to rise. Prices will not be certain to fall until the reduction in demand is sufficient to cause production to be less, perhaps rather substantially less, than current capacity. When the economy is regulated by countervailing power, the relation of current levels of production to the current capacity of plant and labour force is of fundamental importance.

As a practical matter, both under the competitive model and with countervailing power, a continuing upward movement of prices requires continuing additions to demand beyond that made available by current production. A government deficit, consumer expenditures from past savings, a boomtime increase in business and consumer bank borrowing, or some combination of all these is necessary to sustain the movement. However, where there is countervailing power the net addition need only be sufficient to hold production at or near capacity. This may not need to be very great. Much of the requisite addition to demand can, indeed, be supplied as a concomitant of the wage and price increases.*

The force of this interaction of wages on prices and prices on wages is partly, but only partly, lessened by the fact that important components of the cost of living – most notably food, and in practice also houseroom and much clothing – are not immediately affected by increased wages. These are set in competitive markets where there is no immediate response by prices to an increase in costs. Thus the effect of wages, via costs on prices and back on wages by way of the cost of living, is not quite as direct as appears at first glance.

* This is evident in the case of wage income and is especially important because the increased wage income in some measure anticipates the price increases which result in its absorptions. Elsewhere in the economy, especially in the management of inventories, the price increase induces or even forces increases in income, the source of which is either corporate dis-saving or increased bank loans.

Nevertheless, we must reckon on a continuing interaction of wages on prices whenever demand is pressing on the capacity of the economy.

### III

In principle, the Keynesian formula can be brought to bear on an excess of demand and on price increases resulting from wage-price interaction. Increased taxes and decreased government spending could reduce demand below the amount that is necessary to carry off the current supply of goods. There is also a possibility that, by restricting bank credit, business expenditures for inventories, plant, and equipment and consumers' expenditures for durable goods can also be reduced. However, apart from some opportunities for the direct control of consumer credit, this is a far less certain way of reducing spending than by increasing taxes and by reducing public expenditures. It is precisely for this reason, as the layman viewing controversies on this agitated subject should be aware, that it breeds such violent disputes. When one is having the greatest difficulty proving his case, he is always tempted to take refuge in the greatest certainty of statement.

The effect of reducing the demand for goods is to make it difficult to increase prices. Increasing living costs, in turn, cease to be a pretext or an occasion for wage demands. And, because employers will have greater difficulty in passing wage increase along in prices to the public, these will be resisted.

There are three difficulties with this policy, none of which hampers its counterpart application to deflation and depression. There is first the ineluctable fact that it runs not with, but against, the current of politics. To decrease government expenditures and especially to raise taxes is politically far less agreeable than the reverse – as a myriad of prophets of the commonplace have emphasized. Beyond this is the fact that, while no one makes money out of a depression – the unvocal *rentiers* and recipients of fixed incomes excepted – inflation is financially to the advantage of important groups in the community. Those whose income moves with prices are, at a minimum, in a protected position and those whose selling prices show a greater than average amplitude of movement gain in real income. In the inflation years of the forties, farmers and recipients of business profits gained greatly in real income. Both are influential. It is not possible for any reputable American to be overtly in favour of inflation; it is a symbol of evil, like adultery, against which a stand must be taken in public however much it is enjoyed in private. In any case, no person of repute can espouse inflation on behalf of his own income. But the best that can be hoped from this moral ban is neutrality. Those who benefit from inflation cannot be counted upon to be militant proponents of the measures that hold it in check.

The second difficulty, which has been already mentioned, is that when demand is augmented by pressure of government requirements for things of high urgency, only half of the Keynesian formula is available for use. And the use of that half is contradictory and even unwise. When the demand that is pressing on the capacity of the economy is for defence or war requirements, it is obviously not possible to relieve this pressure by reducing these government expenditures. The spending that is causing the pressure on demand is for something of a higher order of urgency even than stability. Inflation that is being caused by defence spending cannot be checked by reducing defence spending.

Thus, in wartime or when war threatens, the government has only taxation or its equivalent at its disposal as a final measure. But this presents problems beyond the obvious ones. The object of an astringent tax policy, as I have just noted, is to make goods hard to sell – to make it difficult for employers to pass the costs of wage increases along to the public. As a further necessary effect, this policy reduces the demand for labour so that employers are not impelled to surrender to all wage demands in order to hold their labour force. In brief, a strong tax policy works by reducing the pressure of production on capacity.

But in different terms, this means that some plant and some labour must be unemployed. This does not happen in competitive industries, like agriculture, where a new equilibrium of supply and demand with full use of resources will promptly be found at a lower price. It is an absolute and inescapable requirement for stability in industries characterized by a generally developed countervailing power. Some slack in the economy is what keeps countervailing power from being converted into a coalition against the public.

In peacetime the unemployment and idle capacity necessary for stability is not probably of great consequence. Such unemployment is not chronic. It need not be great in amount, as we have now discovered. Those whom it affects, apart from the fact that they are now protected by social security and public welfare assistance, can normally expect re-employment in their regular occupation within a reasonably short time. They can as individuals, with reasonable luck and diligence, find re-employment in another occupation at any time. We are not dealing here with the hopeless idleness of the thirties.

Given the imperatives of defence or of war, however, no unemployment can be afforded – or at least it will not be afforded. There is certain to be pressure to use the labour force and industrial plant to capacity. The effect of this is to rule out the possibility of achieving stability by high taxation. Although few forms of sport are more favoured with us, it is impossible to ride two horses in opposite directions at the same time.

These matters have been the subject of serious misunderstanding by those who presume to educate. Economists have regularly urged that taxation – drastic taxation – is both the sufficient and the only remedy for inflation in an economy which is under the pressure of wartime requirements. There have been few doubts on the matter. Evidently a policy requiring so much self-discipline and inflicting so much pain cannot be wrong.

Businessmen, whose attitudes towards taxation may be conditioned somewhat by the weight of their own taxable liability, have not shared the economists' enthusiasm for this policy. Their disposition has been to suggest that the answer to inflation is more production. This is even more specious. When additional goods are produced, additional income, in the form of wages or other payments, also becomes available to buy them. Except for the part of this income that is taxed away or saved, there is an increase in demand to match the increase in supply. But more important, it will now be clear that the pressure of production on the capacity of the industrial plant and labour force, with its effect on the operation of countervailing power, leads directly to inflation. Increased production may be an imperative, but imperative efforts to increase production, so far from being a cure for inflation, are a cause.

When production must be maximized, as under the threat of war, the only alternative to open inflation is to remove to central authority the power of decision over prices and wages. There is no alternative, however unpalatable this course may seem. Then wage and price controls rather than the now intolerable slack in the economy – the margin of unemployed men and plant which can no longer be afforded – keep wages from acting on prices and prices from acting on wages. This is the function of these controls. There is still a strong case for taxation. To the greatest extent possible it is important to prevent redundant demand from building up behind the controls. The only difference is that, with the controls, taxes are no longer expected to achieve ends that are inconsistent with maximum production.

In recent times, when under the pressure of wartime requirements, the United States and virtually all other western countries have used controls. There has been a curious sense of guilt in doing so. In fact it was the only course of action. The indirect controls are inconsistent with maximum output. Open inflation, the remaining possibility, has even more serious consequences. It has damaging social and political effects. In particular it is damaging to the effectiveness and integrity of government and it is destructive of schools, colleges, churches, charitable institutions – in fact of all of the amenities which Western man has so laboriously built up and which permit him to describe himself as civilized. It rewards the grossest and most material of talents. No democracy that has experienced a severe or a long-continued inflation has survived wholly intact. But inflation is also inimical to production. It rewards equally the man who produces and the man who holds resources out of production for their appreciation in money value. It draws resources from where they are most needed to serve the wants of those who have most profited. So it, also, is inconsistent with maximum useful production.

IV

The problem of restraining an excess of demand, when the latter is occasioned by other than military spending, is in principle much simpler. Then the full resources of fiscal policy remain at the disposal of the government. Public expenditures can be reduced because increased expenditures are not an even higher objective of policy. By reducing expenditures and raising taxes the requisite slack can be created in the economy. And this can be afforded. Price stability and the rehabilitation of the normal operation of countervailing power is more important than squeezing the last bit of production from the economic system.

All this is relatively easy in principle. The practice may still be difficult. Modern political attitudes and voting behaviour are rather sensitive to unemployment, even minor unemployment, as a wealth of recent evidence suggests. The action that is required – the reduction of spending and the increase of taxes – is not politically agreeable. Action may be required at a time when the budget is balanced and showing a surplus. To those who have accomplished the considerable intellectual feat of resisting modern fiscal policy, this will seem sufficient indication that nothing need be done.

There is finally the special problem of the boom. As noted, a plausible counterpart of a peacetime surplus of demand is an outbreak of speculation. This, indeed, may be much more important than the increase in prices in general. Beyond a certain point, roughly the point where preoccupation with short-run capital gains replaces calculations of prospective earnings, the boom cannot be checked. It can only be reversed for, once those who are in the market for short-run gains lose hope of getting them, their efforts to realize them will bring down the market. In this situation there will always be fear on the part of those in authority that steps to check the boom may have widespread repercussions, as indeed they may.

It is improbable that any modern government can have a policy of simply standing aside in face of a speculative boom any more than it could follow such a policy in face of a depression. In both instances, however, there are many opportunities for simulating action without in fact doing very much. Postponement is also a policy that can be richly exploited. There will be many temptations for there will always be many to advise that all is well. Nothing so develops the latent fatuousness in a community as a speculative boom. It is probable that it presents an unsolved problem of restraint.

v

I have argued that capitalism, as a practical matter rather than as a system of theology, is an arrangement for getting a considerable decentralization in economic decision. An examination of the prospects for capitalism – of the substance of the fears which the early chapters of this book dug out of the books and the boardrooms – becomes, in the last analysis, an examination of the prospects for decentralized decision. A major danger to decentralized decision has now been isolated. It does not come from depression. Indeed a tendency in this direction must be counted a positive strength. The threat resides in inflation and boom.

Given war or preparation for war, coupled with the effect of these on the public's expectations as to prices, there is every likelihood that the scope for decentralized decision will be substantially narrowed. It is inflation, not deflation or depression, that will cause capitalism to be modified by extensive centralized decision. The position of capitalism in face of this threat is exceedingly vulnerable. This is not a matter of theory but of experience. In the autumn of 1950 a secondary military operation in a country thousands of miles away was sufficient to bring about a wholesale centralization. Authority over prices and wages as well as numerous other matters was removed from businessmen to the federal government. A few months of inflation accomplished what ten years of depression had not required. For twenty years Americans who hold to the doctrine of the malignant state had suspected that New Dealers and Fair Dealers had in mind some such design for American capitalism. In the event the action was forced on the Administration by an essentially conservative Congress.

The threat of peacetime inflation is less precise. It could bring an upsurge in prices and pressure for controls. The greater likelihood is a more limited speculative development with deflation and hardship when the inevitable reaction comes. Of the effect of this on the present scope for private decision little can be said. Such a misfortune would not be good for the reputation of private capitalism. In the past such deviate behaviour has ordinarily led to some narrowing of the scope for private decision. It might be considerable.

In any case there is no doubt that inflationary tensions are capable of producing a major revision in the character and constitution of American capitalism. Policy against depression, about which conservatives have been so deeply disturbed for so long, has little effect on essentials. Policy against inflation has a profound effect. Boom and inflation, in our time, are the proper focus of conservative fears.

# INDEX

## Index